Motivating students

Routledge Education Books

Advisory editor: John Eggleston
Professor of Education
University of Keele

Motivating students

Ruth M. Beard
Professor of Education, University of Bradford

and
Isabel J. Senior

Routledge & Kegan Paul
London, Boston and Henley

First published in 1980
by Routledge & Kegan Paul Ltd
39 Store Street,
London WC1E 7DD,
9 Park Street,
Boston, Mass. 02108, USA and
Broadway House,
Newtown Road,
Henley-on-Thames,
Oxon RG9 1EN
Printed in Great Britain by
Redwood Burn Limited
Trowbridge & Esher

British Library Cataloguing in Publication Data

Beard, Ruth Mary
    Motivating students. – (Routledge education books).
    1. Motivation in education
    2. Achievement motivation
    3. College Students – Great Britain – Psychology
    I. Title   II. Senior, Isabel J.
    370.15'4   LB1065   80-40534

    ISBN 0 7100 0594 6

Contents

Preface

This book owes its existence to Professor E.G. Edwards, Vice Chancellor of the University of Bradford until he retired in 1978, and to members of University Committees who decided that a Research Assistant should be appointed to assist in an enquiry mainly into examinations.

Following interviews with staff and students in some Schools of Engineering and Science, and study of the literature, the Research Assistant, Isabel Senior, and I decided that it would be wise to concentrate on the problems and views of first-year students. Students' experiences during this year often contribute decisively to ultimate success, or to failure or voluntary withdrawal. We were surprised to find that there were few studies of students' initial experiences and their consequences. Thus, although this book deals with assessment, including examinations, we have also considered other factors which contribute to academic success: the students' characters, courses they join, the total environment at university or college, interactions with teachers and teaching methods. We are grateful to the many staff and students at Bradford who agreed to be interviewed or supplied information about courses, examinations and teaching, in particular Professor Carl Hanson and Professor Eric Lees who as Heads of Schools gave us considerable support.

We owe thanks, also, for permission by Professor Noel Entwistle, Dr John Wilson, and their publishers, Hodder & Stoughton, to reproduce table 9.4 from 'Degrees of Excellence'. We are grateful to Dr David Grugeon who not only permitted us to quote freely from the Draft Unit on Course Tuition which he edited in 1972 but also drew our attention to the more recent publication, 'Teaching for the Open Uni-

versity', edited by Dr D. Sewart.   In addition we wish to
thank a number of authors who replied helpfully to queries
about publications.

Lastly our warmest thanks are due to Gladys Claridge,
who with remarkable speed and accuracy typed numerous
reports and drafts for us during the years of the enquiry
and, finally, the entire text of this book.

Ruth M. Beard

Chapter 1

What is motivation?

VIEWS OF TEACHERS AND STUDENTS

When teachers in higher education discuss their problems, a
fairly frequent complaint is that students are not motivated.
Teachers who say this explain that students lack an urge to
work independently, applying themselves only if external
pressures are exerted. When invited to give examples or
to expand their comments, they may add that students these
days are not interested in the courses they have selected
but simply 'want a qualification and a good job'. Or they
may cite instances when they attempted to interest students
in new developments in their field, only to have them inquire
'Is this for the exams?', and if it was not, to pay little
attention.

Such teachers account for the enthusiasm of part-time
students working for degrees in the Open University by their
relative maturity. Older students, they say, have had time
to find out where their interests lie, and experience has
shown them what is important. If attention is called to the
sound attitudes and hard work of younger students in some
medical schools, colleges of education, or engineering departments, they comment that students who have already decided on a career can be expected to work well; it is those
straight from school, having little idea how they may use a
qualification, who are most often a problem.

Since the older teachers claim that this was not the case
when they were undergraduates twenty or more years ago,
and since comments concerning lack of motivation are fairly
common, it could be that there are genuine differences between the present generation of students and that of their
parents of earlier generations.

1

However, discussion with students suggests that there are many ways in which the enthusiasm of beginners in higher education can be diminished, or in which initial doubts may soon be turned into certainty that a course is not for them. The course may prove boring, too difficult, diffuse and ill organized, or irrelevant to their needs and interests. Students may find that the examinations at the end of the first year require cramming of information from lectures and books, leaving little time – and offering no reward – for originality or deeper study of their subject.

This book, therefore, is concerned with questions relating to the nature of motivation amongst students taking higher studies and how it may be fostered. We shall consider whether certain kinds of students are more motivated than others, and if so, in what ways and why. Do some courses, assessment systems or teaching methods increase or diminish motivation, or is it more a matter of persons and their attitudes? Are initial experiences influential in determining students' subsequent success in, and enjoyment of, a course? Is enough known for us to recommend ways of selecting students who will work independently and enthusiastically, or of promoting such behaviour in all, or almost all, of those students who are selected?

As we consider each question, or series of questions, we shall make recommendations, based on students' responses in interviews and on evidence from research and inquiry by teachers or psychologists so far as this is available.

The amount of research having a direct bearing on students' motivation and growing independence in study is still small. In general, students' learning has been explored in relation only to information and skills gained, or growth of comprehension, as a result of different teaching methods. The effects of courses and institutions on students have been explored extensively in the United States of America but so far rather little in Britain. And it is astonishing – since it is often asserted that initial experiences can be important in determining students' subsequent attitudes to a course – that practically no reports of investigations into the consequences of initial experiences can be found. In many departments, of course, teachers discuss students' initial experiences with them with a view to making improvements the next year, but what they have discovered and the steps they have taken remain unknown to other teachers in their field.

Competition motivates only those students who feel that they have a chance of doing well. Those who think they have no chance simply give up

VIEWS OF PSYCHOLOGISTS

In contrast to the teachers, psychologists have considered
and investigated motivation in some depth, although, charac-
teristically, members of different schools of thought describe it in different ways. Members of the cognitive school
tend to speak in terms of drives, goals and needs of the
learner which prompt him to action, whereas those of behav-
iourist/associationist orientation talk of an increase in the
level of responding of an organism following reinforcement
in a situation, such as some incentive or intrinsic satisfaction.

Lewin (1952), for instance, speaks in terms of students'
expectations and goals. In his view it is the various groups
to which an individual belongs that determine his beliefs and
ideologies and consequently his motivations. He stresses
that learning feeds on success; a person's goals and
achievements are limited to what he thinks he can achieve.
Where parents or teachers often act as if they think children, or students, are lazy or dull, they may come to accept
this evaluation of their motives and abilities. Unless motivation is extraordinarily high, a continuous succession of
failures discourages the learner of any age, possibly to the
point where frustration blocks further effort. This is a
reason why the effect of many tests may be worse than none
at all.

Lewin considers that motivation is strongest in situations
that are puzzling. In his view, therefore, teachers are
misled if they feel that each unit of work, or each class
period, should end with a full resolution of whatever issue
was under study. Although these teachers may feel it is
better to tell students 'right answers' than to leave them
'unsatisfied', he considers that no policy could be more
effectively calculated to destroy sustained motivation.
Indeed they may be in error on two grounds, for it is well
known that interrupted tasks, if considered worthwhile, are
considerably more likely to be remembered and returned to
than completed ones.

Bruner's (1966) rather different view is that learning is
an intrinsic motive which finds both its source and its
reward in its own exercise. Thus lack of motivation is
likely to become a problem only when learning is imposed on
the learner, for it may then fail to enlist his natural curiosity, seeming irrelevant or inappropriate to his needs; or
the learning required may be at a level which makes

achievement of competence impossible. Bruner suggests
that individuals have a need for competence models, not to
imitate - but rather to incorporate in an internal dialogue;
in this way a student may assimilate the different standards
of admired teachers partly as his own.

He suggests, too, that human beings have the need to respond to others in a community of learning, acquiring its
values, skills and ways of life in so far as they are able.
Since no one member of a community can master all its com-
petencies, each will make different contributions to the
whole; consequently there cannot be a full involvement of
individuals unless they are allowed to develop specialized
roles. Thus his view of education approximates to the
'give and take' of a seminar in which discussion is the
vehicle of instruction, and this precludes any requirement
that every student in a group should learn the same things.

In contrast to 'cognitive' psychologists, those of the be-
haviourist school speak more of providing motivation through
incentives and rewards with a view to establishing behaviours which may in time become their own reward. Spence
(1959) comments that a primary function of teachers is inculcating interests and 'goals' in students through use of
'rewards' of various kinds. Subsequently incentives may
be provided by verbal cues which act as 'secondary reinfor-
cers' such as 'I'll get an A for this', or 'If I do this well,
I may get a better degree'. On the face of it, this seems to
be the kind of motivation which prompts students to ask 'Is
this for the exams?' instead of gaining their satisfaction in
mastery of subject matter and its applications, or in questioning established results. Nevertheless, it is possibly
valuable if it assists in inculcating good study habits or in
fostering interests which can be further developed in the
right kind of environment.

THE ACHIEVING INDIVIDUAL

During the last twenty-five years or so, psychologists have
given considerable attention to an aspect of motivation which
they term 'need for achievement', usually abbreviated to
'n'ach'. They have investigated in particular how it develops in families.

Rosen and D'Andrade (1959), in a study of boys who
scored high or low in tests of n'ach, found that the parents
of boys who were highly motivated to achieve set higher

standards for their sons than did other parents and generally anticiapted better performance. These parents, especially the mothers, more readily reinforced their son's success in difficult tasks with praise and displays of affection
but punished failure to reach goals that they set. Other
psychologists, at about the same time, confirmed that the
young sons of mothers who rewarded their striving to
achieve already displayed a high degree of achievement
striving in nursery school. In the former study, fathers
of boys high in n'ach were not excessively dominant and did
not interfere with their son's decison-making. In the case
of girls it was mainly their father's praise and reward of
their intellectual accomplishments – whilst avoiding adverse
criticism of their efforts – which led to high achievement.

In a study of eight-year-old boys, McClelland (1958) reported that mothers of boys already showing high n'ach expected their sons from an early age to know their way
around the city, and to be active and energetic, to try hard
things for themselves, to make their own friends and to do
well in competition. Mothers having sons low in n'ach, reported more restrictions; their sons were not allowed to
play with children their parents had not first approved or to
make decisions for themselves.

Moss and Kagan (1961), who studied behaviours of children between the ages of three and fourteen years, found
that mothers who showed much affection to their sons in
their earliest years but soon tried to accelerate their performance, tended to have adult sons motivated to high
achievement and concerned with intellectual competence;
the adult pattern of n'ach was already established by six
years.

These characteristics of families are borne out by
McClelland in his interesting book 'The Achieving Society'
(1970). In this he explores characteristics of individuals,
families and larger cultural groups in countries and communities which have enjoyed exceptional commercial success,
whether or not this was accompanied by other cultural
achievements. One of his conclusions is that in 'achieving
societies', high drive to succeed is associated with a philosophy or religion calling for independence of mind. The
Protestant Reformation, for instance, fostered a character
type having a more vigorous spirit with a shift to greater
self-reliance than that found in Catholic societies. A
Protestant saw his prime responsibility as doing his best in
the occupation to which he was called, gaining satisfaction

from a sense of having worked hard and done his job well. He relied less on an institutionalized church and put a greater stress on literacy to enable all adherents to read the scriptures. Since the beliefs of minority groups such as Calvinists, Quakers and Wesleyans prevented them from enjoying the fruits of their labour they tended to re-invest wealth, so becoming richer. Even today there is still a contrast in wealth between Protestant and Catholic countries, as McClelland shows.

Characteristics of students and children high in n'ach have been reported in a number of studies. They are relatively independent of adults, less likely to conform to the opinions of their peers in social situations, better able to work under delayed reinforcement conditions, and prefer moderately difficult tasks to easy or very hard ones (Parke, 1969). In the case of children expectations of success and belief in their own responsibility for success affects how long they try in difficult tasks (Crandall et al., 1960). In addition, those high in n'ach engage in energetic, innovative activity; they work hard only when there is some challenge in a situation. Thus they do not care for routine tasks, preferring tasks which require a degree of 'mental manipulation', originality or a new angle of approach for a successful solution. As soon as such an individual solves a problem he loses interest in it. He therefore constantly seeks novelty or new solutions to old problems. If he is a student, it follows that too much time given to revision or to routine exercises may drive him to withdraw from a course.

In situations evoking conformity, these individuals may refuse to co-operate. However, they are as willing to work for a group as for themselves since this, too, can provide a feeling of achievement. Nevertheless their motive is not to gain satisfaction through affiliation. Although they respond to feedback as to how their group is succeeding in a task, they show no interest in appeals - or information - relating to feelings and attitudes of the group.

Psychologists say that choices of courses to study and of careers seem to be made as a joint function of occupational prestige, an individual's need for achievement and of class status. Since business is an 'easy' or 'low-status' ambition for boys from prosperous homes, a likely ambition of those high in n'ach is to become research scientists. Boys from lower-middle-class and working-class homes, if high in n'ach, may find business a challenge, perhaps enjoying the opportunities and risks of building up businesses of their own. Thus, granted that a student high in n'ach sees higher education as relevant to his ambition and finds the course he chooses sufficiently stimulating, he can be expected to do well.

It may be expected that boys from lower-middle and working-class homes will be found in greater numbers in vocational courses, whereas those from more affluent homes, whose parents are in professions, will be more likely to select pure sciences or arts.

Interestingly, there is no really useful test to enable teachers to predict academic attainment, or to measure academic motivation. Perhaps this is because it consists of an interaction of a number of factors - high n'ach on the part of the student, suitability of course content and teaching methods and the student's views of what are appropriate goals for him. As we shall see, students' goals, or orientations, differ widely.

STUDENTS' ORIENTATIONS

Studies of students show that the way they see their university experience differs and that this affects the way they work and the kinds of activities they engage in. Many such studies have been made in the United States.

Overall - including less numerous studies in Australia and England - five different orientations have been identified although, of course, many students to not clearly belong to any one of these. The five may be classified as vocational, academic, social-intellectual or liberal, nonconformist or reformer, and collegiate or social-fun. (McKevitt, 1969; Katz and Katz, 1968; La Nauze, 1940; Cohen and Toomey, 1973.)

Students having a mainly vocational orientation tend to be found in vocational and science courses. They are more interested in work which contributes directly to a qualification and a successful career than in fundamental values; they may well not share the enthusiasm of academically oriented teachers unless these can be seen as contributing to success in examinations. They are also unlikely to be spontaneously interested in the possibilities a university offers for a liberal education through discussion with students in different specialities or participation in a wide range of activities.

Students having academic, social/liberal and reformer or

nonconformist orientations are normally good students; the latter two groups, particularly, see the wider implications of their studies. The academic student is interested in his subject for its own sake and has the capacity to tackle independently and successfully both course work and examinations. The social or liberally oriented student is a good mixer who takes part in university life outside the classroom; he is likely to enjoy discussion methods and other work in groups. The reformer or nonconformist spends a considerable amount of time thinking about and discussing social and political reform and wishes to discuss the social implications of his studies. Each of these groups is willing to work hard and may give of their best in assessment methods, such as projects or long essays, which allow them to pursue their own interests in depth. They may also be critical of narrowly conceived teaching or assessment.

Students having a purely social or 'fun' orientation tend to spend most of their time in non-academic activities. They are often from affluent homes and may come to university primarily to enjoy themselves. They are not given to spending much time in solitary study and therefore tend to perform poorly.

Cohen and Toomey (1973) found that role orientations seemed to be influenced to some extent by past experience in addition to current conditions. Whilst students of social sciences scored higher on the reformer role orientation than did students of life science, physical science or engineering, those in the three latter categories who had experienced full-time employment scored higher on the reformer role than did those lacking this experience.

Students living in university halls scored higher in the two social orientations than did students in industry or those living at home or alone in lodgings. Changes in students' role orientations showed that, in general, initially chosen roles were accentuated during university experience, both the reformer and the social role orientations diverging from the vocational and academic role orientations.

Since it is safe to assume that the great majority of teachers in higher education have an academic role orientation, it seems probable that they may be less than satisfied with students very differently orientated. Nevertheless, these students - apart perhaps from individuals maintaining exclusively a 'fun' orientation - may have much to offer in their careers. Indeed Liam Hudson's findings (1970) show that a number of famous men made indifferent students, possibly because they did not work hard at university.

Since it seems unlikely that students' orientations will be substantially altered it may be wise to consider how best to approach students in order to promote their maximum efforts. The academic student will seek a competence model among his teachers; socially orientated students may prefer work in groups, and should profit from it if it is well structured and organized; the vocationally orientated will look for usefulness and relevance in his intended career. Even the energies of the fun-lover may be enlisted by enthusiastic teaching and stimulating methods, and he, too, is likely to respond to the influence of work orientated groups; whilst, if the behaviourists are right, he may learn to modify his orientation through use of appropriate rewards.

If teachers fail to respond to students in these ways, inevitably some of them are likely to withdraw or to do poorly.

Chapter 2

Learning and motivation*

PROBLEMS OF FIRST-YEAR STUDENTS

'Enquiry into student progress', published by the University Grants Committee in 1968, drew attention to the large number of undergraduates who had left university by the end of the first year of their course. The majority were recorded as doing so for 'academic reasons' such as the unsuitability of the course or examination failure, but it is likely that in many cases this official explanation is a convenient shorthand which masks a multitude of diverse experiences. Initially the pressures experienced at university or college may be social rather than academic; institutions and departments vary in their academic requirements of incoming students, but all such students must face the personal and interpersonal problems of settling in, finding friends and establishing a way of life in a new environment. Their capacity for dealing with these problematic matters will depend upon individual attributes and previous experience, and may be moderated or reinforced by early interactions with those who occupy established positions in the new environment.

In a study of college of education students, Cohen (1972) rated students on the basis of Cattell 16 PF scores as having either high or low anxiety. During the fourth week of their first term the high-anxiety group reported significantly greater numbers of problems than did the low-anxiety group, in the areas of personal and social relations, health, relations with boyfriends or girlfriends, morals and reli-

* Much of this chapter was printed as an article in the 'Bulletin of Educational Research', 13 (1) 1977.

gion, and adjustment to college work. The low-anxiety group reported a moderately high number of problems only in connection with the last mentioned area at this time. By the end of the first year at college the number of problems reported by both groups had diminished; both groups at this stage most often reported problems of adjustment to college work. Thus this study indicates that while the most persistent problems among first-year students are work-related, in the first term other problems may loom much larger for students of an anxious disposition. In his discussion of the results Cohen points out that 'an examination of the actual problems that students identify in each of these areas suggests that one important facet of their overall anxiety relates to their feelings of self-esteem' (p. 622).

As a result of extensive studies at Birmingham University, Wankowski (1973) has emphasized adjustment to academic work as the area in which lecturers and tutors may do most to assist the settling-in of new students. He found that the abrupt change in teaching and learning styles between school and university tended to diminish the academic competence of all but the most independent students, and that this often led to a loss of personal confidence as well. For some students the effects of pronounced initial disorientation persisted throughout the course, those suffering in this way tending to obtain lower degree classes than students coping successfully in the first stages.

Wankowski particularly recommends that university staff take steps to moderate academic anxiety by adopting a more 'teacher-dependent' mode of teaching in the transitional period. This would include smaller lectures, more frequent contact between lecturers and students outside lectures, far more 'feedback' to students on submitted work, clearly formulated objectives, a greater variety of approaches to teaching and of methods of assessment which are clearly explained to students, and discussion with students of their specific learning difficulties. The evolution by students of independent ways of working would be encourage at a pace that suited the individual.

Other studies of first-year students reinforce this view of the need for a transitional period between school and university ways of working. For example, in a study of physics students at Surrey University, O'Connell et al. (1970) reported that it was particularly those students who had come straight from school who needed the first term almost wholly as an adjustment period, catching up with the actual work during their Christmas vacation. Students who had taken their A-levels at technical college (perhaps because they did not fit in at school) and who as a result had experience of more impersonal modes of teaching, seemed to fit into university life much more quickly.

INTRODUCTORY STAGES IN HIGHER EDUCATION

Whilst these factors operate throughout a student's career, their recognition may be vital during the introductory stages at university or college and perhaps throughout the first year. The saying 'well begun is half done' recognizes the importance of initial experiences at a popular level. Although introductory sessions for first-year students in universities are fairly common and special provision is often made to help them during the year, surprisingly the consequences are rarely systematically explored. Perhaps one reason for this is that teachers providing the sessions are too familiar with the existing system to perceive all of a students' initial problems and uncertainties.

At Bradford University we have been seeking published studies relating to introductory courses and experiences; in this we have had little success. In addition we have been talking with staff and students in some schools of the university to find out what provision is made for first-year students and how they fare as a result of it.

Normally, introductory sessions compete for students' attention with many other novel experiences. Some students will misunderstand, or miss the relevance of what is being said however clearly presented and well co-ordinated the sessions are. A student who, for example, is still coping with the immediate problem of finding somewhere to live may have little time or energy to absorb the guidelines to work offered in the first few days. Many Bradford students indicated that they spent several weeks checking information about assessment, work requirements, tutoring systems and so on with one another, and asking questions in tutorials, before they felt confident that they knew 'how things worked'.

Introductory sessions are probably most important for establishing channels of communication. Since individuals vary in the rate at which they become acclimatized to life and work at university, the process of assisting their approach to their studies will need to continue throughout the

first year.   An induction week that is followed by moving
straight into a heavily timetabled, ongoing pattern of work
with little or no opportunity for continued personal contact
between staff and students does little to establish students'
confidence.
   With these provisos, there are four areas which deserve
consideration in view of findings from research and inquiry:
1   use of activities which help students rapidly to get to
    know each other and their teachers,
2   early diagnosis of, and assistance with, difficulties or
    areas of ignorance,
3   aid with study methods and use of the library through
    practical activities,
4   provision of information about the purposes of the
    course, either in the form of practical experience, or in
    written form spelling out its aims, methods of assessment
    and how the teaching will be structured.
We will consider these in order.

1 Getting to know students and teachers

One of the reasons why anxiety is reduced and confidence is
gained as courses progress is that students get to know
their peers sufficiently well to seek help with difficulties
and to discuss their work.   Unless special activities are
used or teaching methods are chosen to bring students together this may take a considerable time.   Students tend to
mix with those they already know, especially early on.   A
student who has now left Bradford described how six of her
school-friends had come to the university, and these were
the people with whom she spent her time although none was
studying the same subject.
   Interviews with students on a course which shares a combined first year with other courses revealed that such students feel a need for some occasions during the first year
when they can meet with just the other students who are pursuing the same course.   Without this they said it would take
a long time to identify fellow students among the many in lectures and practicals.   They commented: 'the feeling of a
group is important.'   Almost all the students who had attended an informal tea-time gathering organized by a tutor for
his tutees warmly commended such an occasion early in the
first term.   For example, one said:
   we really got to know everybody in our group, went round

and saw where everybody was from and everything ... I enjoyed it very much. It certainly set us at ease - and if you did have a problem you wouldn't mind going to see him at all. It was informative as well about the staff, and I certainly learned a lot about the structure of the course itself.

Getting to know teachers is just as important as getting to know fellow students, although it clearly takes longer. Many students have been used to working in small sixth forms with teachers they know well; in contrast, a large university department may seem overwhelmingly impersonal. If so, work may be seen as simply a bureaucratic require- ment. One first-year student described the way in which personal contact fostered his motivation to work: 'If you lose the personal aspect altogether that can put you off trying to work. You've got to have respect for a person - if you have then you feel more obliged to do the work.'

For these reasons, activities in small groups during in- troductory sessions or in the early weeks of a course can be beneficial. These may take the form of obtaining infor- mation in the library, discussing and solving problems, dis- cussing with course tutors work students are about to under undertake and what they expect, or hope, to gain from it. Such activities serve to break the ice, to expose some dif- ficulties which can be dealt with promptly, and to lay foun- dations for future co-operation.

2 Diagnosis and treatment of difficulties

Unfortunately students may be ill prepared for the course they have chosen; in some instances this is due to inade- quate or misleading information as to the content of the course. There seems to be insufficient active encourage- ment to students to prepare themselves further before enter- ing university. In a study of mathematics students at three universities, Cornelius (1972) quotes students' com- ments on difficulties of these kinds. One student said: 'I would have liked a book-list which would have enabled me to find out a little about what I was to expect in university maths. This is the main reason why I did not do any work during the summer.' However, another student commented: 'One word and two word sentences do not mean much to a sixth former, particularly if he doesn't understand what it means, "Algebraic structures" for example.' Where book-lists were provided, a student could say: 'Book-lists were very bad - some books were no longer in print, others unobtainable.' Since an inquiry at Surrey University (O'Connell, Wilson and Elton, 1969) showed that science students had a knowledge of mathematical facts and formulae sufficient as a basis for university work, but that they were weak in concepts and ideas, some preliminary work could therefore have been valuable.

Students differ in skills and knowledge depending upon what A-levels they have studied with which examining boards, and on their preferences for different ways of working. In an attempt to overcome the effects of different entry levels, many courses commence with what is for some students a fairly lengthy period of revision. At Bradford many students have made comments on this aspect of their first-year course, such as 'It was utterly boring and was a pointless course. I was doing six option courses three of which I had done at A-level', or less severely, 'It seems to be recapping a lot of A-level stuff'. The latter student, who unlike the former has not withdrawn, subsequently made the point 'I suppose with this course they can't assume anything because people have done different A-levels and this sort of thing'.

If it should be supposed that the best solution is systematic revision, whether students like it or not, the findings of Beard, Levy and Maddox (1964) suggest that this may result in students well qualified at entry redirecting their attention to social activities with consequent fairly permanent deterioration in their academic achievement. Since any class dealing with A-level material in a predictable fashion is likely to be unstimulating for most of the students involved, a more flexible solution to this problem seems desirable. For instance, it is encouraging to read a paper by Taylor and Hanson (1969) who found that a one-week pre-college maths workshop led to significantly higher grades for those who attended than for controls who were initially rated more able, and that their attrition rate was lower. Perhaps it would be a more effective use of an introductory week if such intensive revision was offered - say, during the mornings - to those who needed it. Another way of dealing with the problem is to offer courses initially at two levels, the lower level including revison but introducing essentials of new subjects, whilst better prepared students take higher level courses studying new subjects in greater detail.

In the Open University the problem is dealt with on an

individual basis, steps being taken to diagnose students'
learning and working difficulties before they begin their
courses. After a meeting with their tutor, students complete some diagnostic pieces of work, and then a further
meeting is held to discuss what steps a student might take to
increase his or her competence. In this way the student is
prepared for beginning the course and is encouraged to feel
accepted by the university as a person with a unique background and certain skills. Difficulties are seen as matters
of concern to both student and tutor, which can be approa-
ched in co-operation.

3 Aid with study methods

Students have described a wide range of study difficulties:
paying attention in lectures, deciding how to take notes and
what notes to take, deciding when and how to use books to
supplement lecture notes, writing essays, concentrating on
private study, deciding on - and sticking to - a level of
working. Many students find themselves continually putting
off the resolve to do something about their study methods,
proceeding on an ad hoc basis with varying degrees of help
from their friends. The result may be that by the end of the
first term they have got seriously behind with work, and feel
unconfident about their ability to improve. Similarly, students who have difficulty finding books or who feel lost in a
large library system may get by initially without resorting to
the library at all, eventually finding themselves at a disad-
vantage.
    Interviews at Bradford suggest that when students first
arrive they are very keen to find out what is expected of
them and how their capabilities compare with others. At
such a time many would actively co-operate in self-diagno-
sis, for example in practising taking notes in lectures: 'It
would be good if we could have an example lecture, when you
can just practise picking out important points, and getting an
example from the lecturer of just what he would have expected you to have got out of his lecture.' Few students would
wish to do away with Freshers' Week but many have suggested that part of the time could be spent on activities like the
above.
    Some teachers and librarians have found effective ways to
assist with study difficulties. Bristow (1970) held seminars
to help mature students to improve reading skills, note

taking and reporting. Students read and summarized
papers or books, describing their findings to the group.
They benefited considerably from comments of their peers
in addition to those of the group leader. At Bradford University, Crossley (1968) used exercises when introducing
students to the library and its use. The exercises resulted
in a higher level of library inquiry and increased use of
inter-library services. Steedman (1974) found that lectures on information sources combined with a literature
exercise received a favourable response from students who
made a much better start in a project than did students not
treated in this way.

In a study designed to increase students' awareness of
the reader's requirements when writing descriptions of
technological equipment, Loewenthal and Kostrevski (1973)
set pairs of students to describe objects to each other.
The group who had this training not only showed superior
ability to a control group in describing a common object but
also gained significantly in performance in the verbal section of Heim's AH5 test of intelligence. Other ways of
helping students in writing experimental reports or essays
have been described by Prosser (1967), Wason (1970) and
Woodford (1972).

4 Knowledge of the purposes of the course

A main cause of complaint by first-year students is that
they cannot see what the purposes of their courses are.
They see, of course, what successive tasks are required of
them as the course unfolds bit by bit; what they lack is any
conception of overall organization or a worthwhile purpose
in what they are doing.

From interviews at Bradford it was clear that presentation by teachers of the aims of each course was highly
valued, whether during formal lectures or in informal tutorial discussions. Both types of presentation were thought to
be necessary and to supplement one another. In a course
where no introductions were given students complained bit-
terly: 'On Monday morning, they could have said what they
were going to do instead of doing it; we walked in there one
minute and were taking down notes the next.' Students
would have liked an introductory lecture from each lecturer,
outlining the scope of his subject and how it related to the
course as a whole. This could include discussion of rec-

ommended books and presentation of work, how that section
of the course will be assessed, comments on library use and
on what the lecturer expects students to get out of lectures.
Such introductions are likely to increase motivation; in
their absence students may get caught out and confused; as
one student explained a few weeks into term:

> from here it's hard to see where all the separate sections
> fit together really. You keep sort of thinking you have a
> better idea and then you find out something else is going
> to happen which you didn't expect.... I only found out
> two days ago that the practical books are going to be
> handed in for assessment which I hadn't heard anything
> about – it would have been nice to know before you
> started.

In addition to outlines from individual lecturers, a simple
general outline of the three or four years ahead, and of the
organization of the department, is valuable. Inevitably
some students will not absorb all the information given at
such a time, since many will not yet have in their minds an
appropriate framework within which to place information.
In one school at Bradford, several students had not understood the function of personal tutors even after their first
meeting with the relevant lecturer; in their minds he was
yet another kind of academic tutor.

One area of information which a general introduction
should aim to communicate is who to see about what; armed
with this a student can begin to place himself and other
people in the department and to act effectively within that
context. Students at Bradford stressed that lecturers
should introduce themselves in their first lectures; otherwise it could take a long time to fit names to faces.

In vocational courses practical experience, even for a
brief period, whether in hospitals for medical and dental
students, schools for intending teachers, industry for engineers, or architects' offices for student architects, seems
to have an informing and motivating effect. For instance,
Steubner and Johnson (1969) found that a group of dental
students who spent two days in surgical wards – where
teaching was minimal but practical experience with all
grades of staff was at a maximum – required less time and
found it easier to assimilate information than did a group
which attended twenty-two lectures during a period of ten
weeks.

Sandwich courses have been designed with this advantage
in mind. In Australia, where students on sandwich courses

have been compared with graduates lacking industrial experience (Davie and Russell, 1975), the former proved superior
in social and academic maturity and in technical prepared-
ness for their future roles.

CONCLUSION

The preceding survey illustrates some important aspects of
students' initial experiences at university. Where these
experiences are particularly bad the result may be rapid
withdrawal, despite a student's desire to continue studying
within a subject area or to gain a degree. Clearly, however, effective and interesting teaching methods will play an
important part in the extent to which students commit themselves to a course, both in the short and the long term.
This is particularly the case where commitment is initially
very tenuous, as for instance with some students who have
accepted places through the Clearing Scheme, or others who
have been talked into applying for university by relatives or
teachers. Contrasting lectures early in an applied course,
students at Bradford made comments like: 'I've had enough
of people dictating notes to me, we got enough of that at A-
level. That sort of lecturing I don't think is very good at
all, because it makes it uninteresting for everybody'; and
'He's a good lecturer, he knows what he's going to say next,
but he puts life and feeling into it and jokes about it; and he
shows us slides which I think break it up - people need a
break from writing all the time.' Tutorials offer different
kinds of learning opportunities, which may be strange at
first but which are generally appreciated: 'You can sit and
discuss something academic with people at your and their
own level - you don't have a chance otherwise. The tutor
starts it off and guides the discussion, but he doesn't run
it.' 'It is through methods that lead students to gaining confidence and taking increasing responsibility for organizing
their own independent work that sixth-formers are trans-
formed into successful university students. For a number
of students this desirable end is decided in the early experiences which their teachers provide.

Chapter 3

Students' characteristics and success in higher education

Twenty years ago, if teachers in universities and colleges had been asked what individual differences influenced success in higher education, they would almost certainly have mentioned differences in intellectual ability and very probably the effects of interests other than academic ones, such as holding office in the Students' Union, which limited the time that students were willing to give to study. Possibly they would have mentioned study methods. In any case, their answers would have depended on observation and personal belief, since few relevant research results were available in Britain.

Today, teachers knowing the growing body of research findings, would be more likely to refer to students' orientations and consequent motivations; to their differing levels of maturity in so far as these influence methods of study and expectations of courses and teachers; to study methods, whether systematic or disorganized; to cognitive styles and personality differences which influence subject choice and may determine how students choose to spend their time; and, in the light of some very recent research, they might speculate on possible influences of physiological differences on levels of arousal, application to study or even on the development of one cognitive style rather than another.

Interestingly, informed teachers today would be less likely to mention differences in ability or intelligence in relation to success, for a number of investigations have shown that in the highly selected populations of British sixth forms and colleges, students who do well are usually no more intelligent on average than those who do poorly.

INTELLIGENCE AND ACHIEVEMENT

It seems that the addition of information consisting of scores
in tests of reasoning, whether verbal or non-verbal (of
which intelligence tests usually consist) adds little, if anything, to the predictive measures already provided, such as
O- and A-level results, teachers' estimated grades and head
teachers' recommendations. Yet, as we shall see in Chapter 8, these together contribute rather poor guidance to selection, whilst attempts to develop more efficient measures
including personality characteristics, though somewhat
better, do not reach the point where potential failures can
be identified.

Savage (1972) reported of students in a medical course
that 'poor' students were as intelligent as 'good' ones and
had as good scholastic ability. They did less well due to
difficulty in reading and note-taking, poorer concentration,
a more inefficient balance between the allocation of study
and social time, in addition to having poorer attitudes to
study. Personality tests showed that they experienced
greater undisciplined self-conflict and were considerably
more extrovert than the good students. The effects of these
characteristics were already apparent in that 'poor' students on average had required more attempts to pass O- and
A-levels.

As a result of studies he made, Hudson (1966) commented
that boys who later won open scholarships to Oxford and
Cambridge differed only very slightly in their mental test
scores from class-mates who went there as commoners, who
went to other universities, or who left school and went to no
university at all. Once they had reached the sixth form,
he noted that the ability of boys to do conventional mental
tests was not closely related to their subsequent achievement - even in examinations, not to mention in later life.

In support of this view he quoted findings in the United
States of America, by Roe (1953) and MacKinnon (1962), who
agreed that men and women of the highest intellectual distinction were not differentiated from their less successful
contemporaries by mental test scores. Indeed, MacKinnon
found that, above an IQ level of around 115-125, conventional intelligence measures had little bearing on subsequent
intellectual achievement. At the time of Hudson's book,
American psychologists were beginning to look at other
characteristics in attempting to identify scientific talent:
for instance, all-absorbing interest in a particular topic,

or even lack of intellectual discipline.   As we noted in Chapter 1, these are characteristics of individuals who have high 'need for achievement', some of whom work hard when interested but idle when they are not.

Measures relating to particular talents and skills, such as verbal abilities or numerical skills, seem to be a little more useful in predicting success, but only in specific subjects.

In Australia, where the range of students' abilities is greater than that of students in England, Silcock (1965) cor-related scores in tests of vocabulary, speed of comprehen-sion and level of comprehension in reading, with scores in subject examinations.   She found significant correlations only for some subjects.   Correlations were significant with all three measures and examination marks in planning, arts, commerce and economics, physiotherapy and law.   Only the vocabulary scores correlated significantly with examination marks in veterinary science, dentistry and medicine, whilst none of the three measures correlated significantly with scores in speech therapy, surveying, agricultural sciences and forestry, pure sciences and engineering; in fact, cor-relations were consistently negative in the case of the last three groups of subjects.   In architecture, there were sig-nificant negative correlations with vocabulary and level of comprehension and a negative, but non-significant, correla-tion with speech.   However, since scores for male and female students were not distinguished, it is possible that these differences were, in part, attributable to predomi-nance of one sex taking a subject rather than to the nature of the subject itself.   It has often been shown that girls and women excel in reading speed and sometimes in reading com-prehension (although not usually in vocabulary), whereas boys and men often excel in spatial and mechanical skills which were not tested in this investigation.

LEVELS OF MATURITY AND STUDENTS' EXPECTATIONS

Teachers at universities sometimes complain that a propor-tion of students, especially in the first year, show limita-tions in their thinking.   At a number of English-speaking universities, teachers have commented on students' belief that theories should be wholly 'right', that a translation should be able to convey the exact meaning of the original, or that experts should never make mistakes.   In the event that an exception to a theory was mentioned, or an expert

was found wrong in one of his views or explanations, those
students became acutely distressed; for when an authority
failed them they did not know what to do other than reject it
completely.   If Bligh is right in his paper on 'The Cynthia
Syndrome' (1977), some students arrive in higher education
from schools where teachers give high marks for information obtained from books or classroom notes, although no
critical faculty is exercised.   Indeed he suggests that some
students pass through university – although with a declining
standard of performance – never realizing that anything over
and above acquisition of information is expected of them!
When they gain a lower-second- or third-class degree, they
decide to teach, and so perpetuate this belief.

There is some confirmation from early sources concerning
limitations in students' thinking.   Perry (1968), who investigated the intellectual development of Harvard undergraduates during four years at college, reported three disting-
uishable stages.   In a first stage, he found that students
expected to find 'right answers' which were known to 'Authority' and saw it as Authority's role to teach these answers
to students.   Gibson (1970) found not only that students of
sociology had a notion that theories and hypotheses were fal-
sified when they had been shown not to apply in certain circumstances, but they also over-generalized experimental
results, failed to recognize particular experiments as building blocks in a wider theory, failed through lack of knowledge to give precise meanings to terms such as 'balance',
'attitude' and 'prejudice', rejected quantitative data, so re-
gressing large tracts of social psychology back into philosophy, and were confused as to what constituted evidence.
He noted a corroborative observation by Peters (1958) concerning students' tendency to seek highly general theories
which were logically impossible, and quoted Veness (1968)
who spoke of 'concepts so lacking in form and content that
they can be conveniently squeezed from the tube in any shape
available.

This seems to correspond roughly with Perry's second
stage in which students were willing to accept alternative
theories and explanations but tended to swing to the ex-
tremes of maintaining that 'everyone has a right to his own
opinion'.   Alternatively, they might come to the conclusion
that there were two or more views which 'Authority' required them to note.   Thus, they either assumed that in the
absence of an absolute Authority no meaningful judgments
could be made, or sought to maintain dependence on Author-

ity and 'absolute truths' since without them they would feel
as one student put it: 'If everything is relative, nothing is
true, nothing matters.'

By the third stage, Perry found that students realized that
knowing and valuing were relative in time and circumstances
and that an individual was faced with responsibility for
choice and commitment in life. Obviously these differences
affect students' learning – those who are still at the first
stage will seek right answers to memorize, whilst those at
stage three will expect to be required to think – weighing one
view against another – and to take responsibility for their
own decisions.

Possibly the distinction of Miller and Parlett (1974) between 'cue-seekers', 'cue-conscious' and 'cue-deaf' students is relevant here. In a study at Edinburgh, 'cue-
seekers' proved to be mature and confident in outlook.
They were aware of, and responded to, the unspoken, implicit requirements and expectations found in every learning
institution (known to sociologists as the 'hidden curriculum').
They found out, for instance, what pieces of set work could
be safely neglected, which topics were of greatest importance, and ways of writing essays or contributing to seminars which gained high marks and the good opinions of their
teachers. They deliberately tried to make a good impression and sought clues as to what would be examined. 'Cue-
conscious' students were aware that a 'hidden curriculum'
existed but did not actively try to discover their teachers'
views and biases in order to improve their chances. 'Cue-
deaf' students were unaware of the hidden curriculum; they
felt that success depended solely on how hard they worked
and how thoroughly they learned the entire syllabus. Thus
their attitudes corresponded with those of students at
Perry's first stage. Significantly, in examinations, 'cue-
seekers' mostly gained first- and upper-second-, 'cue-conscious' lower-second-, and the 'cue-deaf' third-class or
pass degrees.

COGNITIVE STYLES

Perhaps, a potentially more interesting variable than 'intelligence' and 'maturity' is that of cognitive style. It has
been found that flexibility scores increase consistently with
level of degree achievement for both sexes, suggesting that
high achievers tend to be less rigid in their attitudes to

tuition and more ready to change (Howell, 1971).   Alternatively, one might see flexibility as arising from ability to
abstract general principles which have numerous applications in a range of situations.   This is a capacity which
most university teachers claim to look for when awarding
first- and upper-second-class degrees.

Another kind of flexibility is seen in 'divergent thinking'
as described by Hudson (1966) and explored earlier in a
variety of its aspects by Guilford (1956).   Whilst admitting
that an individual may think in convergent and divergent
ways on different occasions, Hudson identified as 'diver-.
gers' those boys who excelled in open-ended test items,
allowing them to think fluently and tangentially, without
examining any one line of reasoning in detail, and as 'convergers' those boys who excelled in intelligence tests requiring a single right answer to each item.   Many arts
specialists, he found, were rather weak at intelligence
tests but much better in open-ended ones; many scientists
were the reverse.   'Convergers' enjoyed thinking about
technical, impersonal matters, liked arguments to be clearly defined and logical and to know when they were right or
wrong.   'Divergers' were not interested in technical matters or in argument which was solely a matter of impersonal
logic.   Predictably, convergers tended to specialize in
pure sciences, whereas divergers favoured arts, law or
business where decisions are made on the basis of proba-
bilities.

It needs to be stressed that many able people are capable
of excelling in both modes of thinking.   Nevertheless, there
are sufficient students and academics having a primarily
'convergent' or 'divergent' orientation to lend some support
to Snow's claim for the existence of two cultures (1959
Reith Lectures).   If, however, it should prove that this
difference does not appear, or is less marked, on the Con-
tinent or in the United States, then it could be argued that
it follows from early specialization in Britain, or from lack
of co-ordinating studies, such as philosophy in sixth
forms.

A parallel distinction made by Hudson (1968), and explored by Parlett (1970), is that between 'syllabus-bound'
and 'syllabus-free' students.   They define the former as
having systematic and conscientious study habits, but showing some anxiety and obsessiveness.   The latter are apt to
demand independence in studying and so may conflict with
tutors; they also like to play around with ideas of their own

and to think out better ways of doing things.   Entwistle and
Wilson (1977, pp. 40-1) report that syllabus-bound students
agree with such statements as: 'I usually study only what I
am required to study; I consider the best possible way of
learning is by completing the set work and doing the required reading; I like to be told precisely what to do in
essays or in other assignments.   They are likely to worry
about an examination or about work that is overdue.   In
contrast, syllabus-free students agree with: I like to play
around with certain ideas of my own even if they do not come
to very much; I tend to learn more effectively by studying
along my own lines than through doing set work; I should
prefer the work to be less structured and organized; often
I try to think of a better way of doing something than is described in a lecture or book.   They question whether the
latter is a single trait, suggesting that the two aspects of
'syllabus-freedom' might prove fairly independent on further
investigation.

PERSONALITY TRAITS AND ACADEMIC PERFORMANCE

Personality traits which have frequently been investigated
in connection with academic success are: anxiety, extroversion-introversion, neuroticism-stability, and 'need for
achievement'.   In addition, creativity and psychoticism
have been tested in a minority of studies.
    In such investigations, anxiety does not refer to the
ordinary worries of students but to a pervasive characteristic underlying a wide range of behaviours as measured by
anxiety scales.   Students whose scores are low tend to be
relaxed individuals who may require pressure from their
teachers, or from an intense interest of their own, before
they will exert themselves.   Those whose scores are high
habitually perform as though under pressure; consequently
they are vulnerable to external pressures and may be preci-
pitated into a state of excessive anxiety which inhibits
effective activity.   For instance, if they are uncertain of
success, or are not clear what is required of them, these
students are apt to break down under examination stresses.
    Personality traits which seem to have considerable bear-
ing on success and failure in higher education are extroversion-introversion and neuroticism-stability.   At the extreme
of the first scale, Eysenck (1970) describes the extrovert as
sociable, liking parties, having many friends, needing com-

pany and disliking solitary study; he also craves excitement,
takes chances and is generally impulsive.   The extreme introvert, on the other hand, is described as a quiet, retiring
individual, introspective, fond of books rather than people,
reserved and distant except with friends.   He tends to plan
ahead, 'looks before he leaps' and distrusts the impulse of
the moment.

On the second scale, whereas the stable person tends to
be reliable, even-tempered and calm, the neurotic is given
to unnecessary worrying, feelings of restlessness, moodi-
ness and general nervousness.   In some investigations,
highly significant relationships have been found between
degree achievement, neuroticism and extroversion-introversion.

Wankowski (1973) found a negative correlation between
degree results and extroversion scores of an order of r =
-.30; amongst female students the negative correlation rose
to -.37 between degree results and neuroticism.   The
highest negative correlation with degree results occurred
where neurotic and extrovert traits combined in females
(r = -.66) and in males (r = -.33).   Thus, in this sub-
sample, high neuroticism combined with extroversion tended
to be inimical to academic success.   It is reasonable to
ask, of course, whether this is caused partly by the way
courses are designed and taught.

As might be expected, neurotic and extroverted male students suffered the greatest losses through failure and voluntary withdrawal.   If they did not withdraw, students with
this disposition tended to get ordinary degrees.   Amongst
female students, however, voluntary withdrawals in Wankowski's samples tended to occur amongst introverts.   In
addition, students who said they could not cope adequately
with their work at the beginning of their first session at university had higher neuroticism scores on average than those
who claimed they could.   Wankowski concluded that students
of either sex who had both neurotic and introverted tendencies were likely to be systematic workers, whereas neurotic extroverts tended to be haphazard.   In his view, persistent anxiety, or neuroticism, is a more powerful influence in
shaping styles of learning and in acquiring attitudes to tuition than is extroversion.   Anxiety, or neuroticism, he suggests seems in some persons to induce states of uncertainty
about work and progress, hostility to school, apprehension
about contact with teachers, compulsive and ritualistic methods of formulating notes, whilst in others it may make for

haphazard methods of study and preference for less formal contacts in tuition.

A somewhat different description of students of high and low attainment is given by Entwistle and Brennan (1971) who used a cluster analysis to identify traits of high and low attainment types. They confirmed the generally rather poor performance of extroverts, including a group described as 'tough minded rationalists', with high social values, who were likely to opt out despite having the ability to complete their courses. Another fairly extroverted group did poorly partly on this account, and partly due to poor entrance qualifications. These were mostly men. Women having poor entry qualifications, and possibly poor examination technique, constituted a third group whose attainments were poor. In contrast, high attainment groups all had good A-levels on entry and high numerical ability. In addition they had high, or fairly high motivation, together with 'good' or average study methods and examination techniques.

It will be noted that these findings seem to run counter to the more general ones quoted initially concerning the rather poor predictive 'ability' of A-levels for degree results. The contradictions may be partly reconciled by a finding of Wankowski (1973), that a positive correlation between A-level and degree results was due largely to the consistently good performance of stable introverts who were usually about a quarter of the student population. Correlation between A-levels and degree results for the remaining students was considerably lower. Thus we may expect correlations to differ with proportions of stable introverts: they will be high if there are many of them – in applied sciences and engineering departments for example – and lower, or negligible where a majority of students is studying, say, the social sciences or humanities.

PHYSIOLOGICAL DIFFERENCES AND LEARNING

A difference between students, which has been explored in Russia within the last few years, is time of maximum physiological alertness. Doskin and Laurent'eva (1974) found that 55 per cent of a sample of more than one hundred students were most alert and performed best between 9 and 14 hours, and 35 per cent between 15 and 24 hours. These they called 'morning' and 'evening' types respectively. For the remaining 10 per cent the time of maximum arousal fluctuated randomly. The authors concluded that 'morning'-type students were best adapted to existing teaching arrangements, whilst 'evening'-type students were relatively disadvantaged; they therefore suggested alterations to the organization of the academic timetable to meet the different needs of these groups. It seems at least questionable, however, whether it is more advantageous to be most fully alert during morning classes or when working independently in the evening. An extensive study exploring the consequences of different kinds of programmes in a variety of subjects and courses in relation to students' alertness might well suggest more complex relationships, if, indeed, any relationship is confirmed.

Conceivably a difference of this kind between individuals casts fresh light on findings relating to effectiveness of student learning at different times of day. Holloway (1966), for example, found that dental students learned less from a lecture during the afternoon than during the morning. If the Russian findings are right, this should be the overall effect; yet study of individual performances would show that two groups of students were affected in different ways. Or, if it should prove that 'morning' types are more likely to choose sciences, whereas 'evening' types favour the arts, Holloway's result would be a consequence of 'natural' selection into dentistry.

A further point of interest here, since students in lodgings cater for themselves, is that it has been claimed that children and adolescents who have breakfast are more successful in studies during the morning. It is possible that 'evening' types are uninterested in breakfast whereas 'morning' types have good appetites then. Consideration of the habits of colleagues suggests that this is often the case. Thus, until the difference has been explored more fully, it seems wise to dispose class activities throughout the day, or, where possible, to allow choice to students as to how they arrange their studies.

The possibility of future physiological control of learning is raised by the finding of Kennet and Cropley (1975) that uric acid levels are lower in highly divergent thinkers than in the less divergent. This led them to speculate that uric acid might be an important biochemical precursor of intellectual functioning.

STUDY METHODS AND LEARNING

Since techniques in study are more easily influenced by advice and guidance from tutors than are abilities, cognitive and learning styles or personality traits, it is perhaps most important that teachers should be aware of student differences in this respect. If students enter higher education with poor study attitudes and skill and have not appreciably improved them by the end of the first term, either they are amongst the most disorientated or teachers have failed to discover and to help them overcome their difficulties. Whichever is the case, the probability of failure is high.

Despite the findings concerning relationships between extroversion, neuroticism and failure, a finding stressing the importance of attitudes to study was made by Wankowski (1973). He found that students with similar study attitudes had comparable levels of performance, irrespective of their personality types. Thus, while 75 per cent of unstable introverts with good study attitudes had good academic performances, 79 per cent of unstable extroverts having similar good attitudes were equally successful. This seems contrary to Eysenck's findings (1957) that extroverts more quickly build up a neural fatigue which acts as a barrier to repetition (reactive inhibition) and condition more slowly, but perhaps this applies only to a majority of extroverts. In addition, extroverts proved superior to introverts in immediate recall but were inferior in delayed recall, i.e. they coded material less effectively into long-term memory (Eysenck, 1970). Thus, if Wankowski's small sub-sample was typical, it seems that extroverts can work as effectively as introverts, conceivably because parents and teachers have insisted on establishing good study methods and the development of sound study skills or, perhaps, due to an over-riding interest of the student in his own chosen field of study.

As we have seen in Chapter 2, means to improve students' performance have been explored in reading, note-taking, writing reports and essays, making oral and written descriptions, examination techniques and use of books and libraries. It is in these respects, and in designing better courses, that teachers can influence students' learning at an early stage in higher education and so ensure that a greater proportion of them succeed in the courses they choose.

Chapter 4

Motivation in relation to environment, course structure and content

TOTAL ENVIRONMENT AND MOTIVATION

The effect on students of the total college or university environment is not normally considered in discussing the selection of students or their motivation and academic performance. However, an American study (Becker, Geer and Hughes, 1968) which has applied a wide sociological perspective to students' activity, points out that what are usually thought to be matters of individual judgment, motivation and action, have in fact a collective character. That is, such matters (including students' academic activities) are formed in a context of extensive and complicated social and work relations, of explicit and tacit demands, obligations and definitions. The view that regards student performance as a simple response to what lecturers offer, or as something which depends solely on the ability and interest of the individual student, ignores these socially structured conditions. Becker, Geer and Hughes found that in an American college academic activities were most fully understood in terms of the assessment a student made as to the value of different activities. Thus, he might weigh the contribution of a particular activity for his overall Grade Point Average, as against the rewards that might be realized through student-organized activities or in personal relationships. In deciding what action to take a student considers all the relevant consequences as he understands them; such consequences include the opinions of other students as well as the judgments of staff, and the effect on grades, in so far as these can be estimated.

This wide sociological perspective stresses the interactions of all participants in the total environment and the relevance of students' diverse goals, many of which may be found to conflict with the institutionalized goal of grades. Another important American study (Snyder, 1973) lays particular emphasis on one aspect of the collectively structured environment, namely the 'hidden curriculum'. As we described in Chapter 3, the concept of a 'hidden curriculum' embraces all the implicit demands of the tuition and assessment systems that students may discover and respond to. To give a crude example, a university or college may profess to be concerned with 'fostering the intellectual development' and 'training the mind' of each student through a study of, say, experimental psychology (and these may be goals of many students on the course), whereas curricular activities pay little heed to or even seem to negate such goals. Students may discover that order, punctuality, neatness, saying the right thing in seminars, doing what they are told, count more than original ideas extensively explored in a laboratory project. Snyder's study points out that in order to make rational judgments about their environment and the influences acting upon them, students need to take cognizance not only of the stated requirements of a course but also of the particular working criteria evolved by each lecturer. Becoming aware of unstated criteria is a social process at which some students will be more adept than others; consequently different students will follow varying 'hidden curricula'.

An elaboration of this point is seen in 'Up to the mark' by Miller and Parlett (1974). In a study of the attitudes of Edinburgh University students to assessment, already mentioned in Chapter 3, they found that students could be placed on different sections of a continuum with respect to their consciousness of and response to the cues of the hidden curriculum.

Miller and Parlett's study shows how the attitudes of cue-deaf students may be turned towards cue-consciousness under the influence of friends more cue-conscious than themselves. Whether cue-consciousness is viewed as a correlate of personality traits or as evidence of cognitive style or neither of these, it seems clear that under present higher education systems the development of cue-consciousness is a realistic adaptive strategy giving the student greater range and control in his interactions in the environment. At the same time there is a clear link between the successful application of cue-consciousness and flexibility of subject area; in a highly inflexible and rigidly-structured domain the cue-

conscious may have little advantage.   In terms of the present discussion, the usefulness of the concept of cue-consciousness lies in its indication of the potential range of
interaction effects in one particular area of student-envir-
onment interaction (assessment) and, deriving from this, of
the different meanings that may be contained in 'student
motivation'.

It is difficult to estimate how the total environment inter-
acts with students' attitudes except by extrapolation from
large-scale interview and observation studies.   Smaller
studies have dealt with only a few aspects such as background characteristics of students, size of institution, or
subject area.

At Bradford University Cohen and Batcock (1969), who
compared matched male and female arts students with
matched male and female science students on entry and
after two years in the university, investigated how their
views on the importance of participation in intellectual and
cultural activities had changed.   On entry female students,
who were in the minority in the university, strongly belie-
ved in the importance of such activities in university life;
however after two years their views had changed to be much
closer to those of their less interested male colleagues.
Further, after two years there was much greater diver-
gence between the views of arts students and science students than previously.

Miller (1976), in an extension of the Edinburgh study
which she made with Parlett (1974), talked to second-year
students about their academic confidence and their feelings
of identification with the department.   Most felt they were
beginning to be known personally in the department and to
understand how things worked.   However an important difference was noted between historians and geographers: the
historians talked much more about wanting to become more
identified with their department, and as a whole seemed to
be less confident.   A tentative explanation for this would
seem to be in the physical size, structure and location of
the respective departments.   Whereas the geography
department 'is located as a separate entity, in an old building away from the rest of the university, with its own cloak-
rooms, library and common room', the larger history
department is housed in a newly built complex together with
other arts departments.   As a result, historians tend to
spend most of their time in the library or at home.

American studies have shown how different kinds of

environment appeal to students having different personality characteristics. The extremely competitive and high-powered programmes at MIT, for instance, appeal to able students from large city schools, whose main orientation is academic or vocational. These students tend to be 'tough' rather than 'tender' in outlook. In contrast small, mainly residential colleges or universities such as Durham and Aberystwyth in Britain are likely to appeal to students having a mixed orientation and to those coming from smaller urban or rural communities. Students who graduate in these universities say how difficult it is to wrench themselves away to take postgraduate studies elsewhere. Other small, residential colleges, including some colleges of education, inspire a similar loyalty in a substantial number of their students.

That admission to medical school involves decisions both on the part of the school and the applicant was recognized by Halstead and Geertsma (1973), who investigated how a group of applicants viewed schools and what they regarded as the most important reasons for their choice of school. Applicants who chose School 'A' cited general considerations such as the school's philosophy, its interest in students and its reputation as the factors most significant in their choice of school. Those preferring another school to 'A' indicated the primary importance of geographical location and clinical and pre-clinical curricula of the school they chose.

COURSES AND STUDENTS' MOTIVATION

The critical effects of courses on students have been mentioned in Chapter 2 where we discussed certain characteristics of courses likely to contribute to failure or success. In this section we shall consider the effects of structure and organization of different kinds of courses on students' motivation. In particular we shall discuss sandwich or co-operative courses and other courses including practical experience, interdisciplinary courses, courses designed systematically for individual study such as those introduced by Postlethwaite et al. (1964) or courses at the Open University, and elsewhere, especially in the sciences, which it is claimed may increase student motivation.

Sandwich courses

Sandwich courses (known as co-operative courses in the United States and Australia) were introduced at Sunderland Technical College (now Sunderland Polytechnic) in 1903 with a view to integrating theory with practical experience and so to increase students' interest and understanding.   Courses of this kind were introduced in Germany at the end of the nineteenth century and in the United States at the University of Cincinatti in 1906.   During this century their number has grown considerably.   Whereas in Britain, in 1959, there were 2,000 sandwich-course students studying for degrees, by 1974 the number had increased to over 33,000, the introduction of technological universities in 1966 being a main cause of the increase (Brunel University, 1974).
    Periods of practical work in vocational courses are common, of course.   This is an essential feature in the training of teachers, doctors, dentists and architects, whilst in language courses students usually spend some time overseas.
    The most extensive study of sandwich, or co-operative courses, has been made by Davie and Russell (1974).   They undertook investigations in universities and colleges in Great Britain and the United States of America prior to studying co-operative courses during their introduction into colleges in Australia.   Industrial organizations in all three countries were also approached for their views.   All the courses alternate classroom and work experience, most commonly in six-monthly periods, but some courses include a year in industry between classroom courses whilst, in the United States, there is also a 'quarter' pattern involving more rapid changes.   Normally it is expected that work experience will be related to the course and integrated with it, the integration being effected through the teaching institution in Britain, but sometimes by an industrial co-ordinator in the United States.
    Whilst it seems certain that practical experience in schools for intending teachers, or overseas experience in industry or university for linguists, will be directly relevant to the college or university course, relevance of industrial experience to engineering or science courses may be more difficult to achieve because industrial requirements vary fairly widely.   Smithers (1976) questions how far the experience is integrated for engineering students in Britain; but his conclusions are based on less extensive studies than

those of Davie and Russell, and he used a narrower range of questions in his investigations.   In 1969, Musgrove reported that in England students who had spent periods in industry on the sandwich course more often found their university studies interesting and appeared to have gained in academic self-confidence.   The conclusions of Davie and Russell (1974, 1975) were that in Britain and America there were a number of benefits to students, employers and to the teaching institutions.   Students had a more relevant course of study leading to greater maturity and better academic performance; the employers gained better relationships with teaching institutions, better prepared staff and the opportunity to play a part in the total educational process; the teaching institutions showed the benefits of better relationships with industry, had more receptive students and more competitive graduates.

Although early co-operative education was centred on engineering, it now includes numerous courses in the whole range of science and technology, business, humanities and social sciences.   In Australia, where co-operative courses have been operating for just over a decade, they are still concentrated in the scientific and engineering fields; perhaps because, as in Britain, they were initiated outside the older universities.

Davie et al. (1975) found that staff and students were satisfied with most of the alternating patterns of study and employment except the alternating quarter pattern common in many American universities.   An appreciable number of academics and students saw this as requiring too many changes of environment and as adversely affecting the continuity of the programme.

During industrial experience liaison by teaching staff was usually considered more effective than that conducted by separate non-teaching staff, but employers gave qualified assent to this view.   It is suggested that a mixed system with placements arranged by administrative staff and liaison undertaken by teachers may be economically and educationally sound.

Davie et al. (1975) comment that the favourable effect of work experience on academic performance suggests that, in designing co-operative courses, the total academic time should be less than that for corresponding full-time courses. Where this policy is adopted – as it is in the United States – then the use of an alternating pattern may lead to marked savings in capital costs.

From a review of earlier work and from studies conducted in the New South Wales Institute of Technology, they conclude that co-operative education has a favourable influence on academic performance in a consistent, although in most instances, not a marked manner. Students in co-operative courses have a lower attrition rate, lower failure rate and higher average marks than comparable students in part-time or full-time courses.

Structured courses for individual study

In the late 1950s and the 1960s, following the development of programmed learning, entire courses were devised in a similar systematic way for individual study. Their growth has been most rapid in the United States of America, but Canada and Australia also have some notably successful courses of this kind, and Britain has a few. Most of them derive from the innovatory work of Postlethwaite et al. (1964) and Keller (1968).

Students are normally supplied with a work book, such as Open University students receive in Britain. This outlines the general aims of the course and the successive aims, objectives and requirements of each section. Where relevant, a tape recorder and tapes, slide cassette or other visual aids and a book of tests may be supplied. Exercises or activities are carefully structured to enable the student to learn unaided the content or skills in each section; the test which follows enables him to find out how far he has been successful. In some programmes objectives are spelled out in great detail, whilst in others only general aims are stated. Some courses include periods of group discussion from time to time, or discussion may be an essential part of certain activities. In all courses teachers are available for consultation, although in correspondence courses this may of necessity be via the post.

Observation suggests that successful courses of this kind wholly involve the students' attention. A visitor entering the room where students are working individually in booths (or less expensive carrels arranged along work benches) will find himself unnoticed. Each student is absorbed in his activities, leaving his place only to collect additional material or to question a teacher. There is a sharp contrast with the apathy and low level of arousal in some lecture rooms. Where study is individualized, the student feels responsible for his progress, he works at his own pace so that he is more likely fully to understand the material.　Tests supply knowledge as to how he is progressing, whilst almost inevitable success reinforces his activity.

In Britain, the main example of this approach, in a number of modified forms, is at the Open University. Courses in the sciences consist of (i) a few lectures viewed on television, mainly to enable students to see their teachers, (ii) course books which outline course aims and objectives and the main content of the course, (iii) tutorial group discussion with other students and teachers from local universities during term, (iv) vacation courses which provide more contact with teachers, and (v) laboratory exercises at home using specially prepared apparatus (more complex laboratory work being kept for vacations).　Experts from the Educational Technology Unit help groups of teachers to plan and to prepare the written courses, and to devise multiple-choice tests and correspondence exercises. The entire course team comments on each contributors' drafts with a view to removing ambiguities and unclear presentation.　In addition, the Educational Technology Unit supplies information to students concerning their progress, and offers feedback to tutors on their performance in teaching and on the value of their comments on students' work.

Whilst it may not always be possible to say just what a course is intended to achieve, the advantages where this can can be done are very evident.　It is of interest that, when the Foundation Science Course was about to begin at the Open University, some science students on receiving the course book wrote to their teachers saying that they did not find the aims and objectives at all helpful and would be glad to know what they should learn.　Evidently they conceived of science as a body of information to be learned from books; they did not think in terms of skills and abilities needed by experimental scientists.　Since the aims had been stated a discussion was initiated which enabled students to amend their expectations in line with those of the teachers.

Discussion with students in various university departments suggests that many of them are not so fortunate. For example, at one medical school, very able graduates supposed that their teachers expected them to learn all the content of their large medical books!　In this instance the teachers were astonished that students could have such a misconception, but it had not occurred to them to discuss with their classes just what they did expect.

Yes to structural cause 'le o.u

That students feel the need for more guidance as to what
they should study, and how to go about it, was shown at a
conference organized and attended by British medical students at Nottingham in December 1972.   They planned a
three-day workshop in which they hoped to learn to spell
out objectives of the curriculum themselves to supply a
basis for discussion with their teachers.   They appointed
consultants (teachers from medical schools, educational
technology units and university teaching method units) who
agreed that they should be sent for when required and asked
to leave when no longer useful.   One group began, on the
second day, to understand how to differentiate long-term
aims from objectives, and chose to write objectives for a
course in community health.   Other groups made an equally
successful beginning.

It was of interest in group discussion at the conference
to find that students from the new schools in Newcastle,
Nottingham and Southampton were generally happy with
their courses since they felt that they knew where they were
going.   Feelings of students from more traditionally organized courses, however, ranged widely from modest enthusiasm to almost total disillusion.   Yet teachers of courses in
which students have become apathetic normally ascribe their
apathy either to poor preparation in school (if they teach
pre-clinical courses) or to the aftermath of swotting for
pre-clinical exams (if they are clinical teachers).   What
we have said indicates that the explanation should perhaps
be sought in the design of courses themselves and the
teachers' skills in communicating with students.

Interdisciplinary courses

Interdisciplinary courses have multiplied in recent years.
Even by October 1976, the Nuffield Foundation Group for
Research and Innovation in Higher Education, in its final
newsletter, no. 7, could report that during its four-year
programme, their newsletters recorded some four hundred
departures from the conventional pattern of lecture-based,
three-year, single-subject courses, assessed by unseen
examination at the end of the final year.   These spanned
the totality of university institutions - sixty in all - and
twenty polytechnics.   In colleges of education where most
of the recently introduced undergraduate courses are interdisciplinary, the number and variety of courses is very

considerable; many, but not all, are interdisciplinary by
virtue of choice amongst units in different subject areas.
It is impossible in a few pages to do justice to their diversity.

The Nuffield Group found little distinction between courses introduced in universities and polytechnics. Greater
concern with degree programmes or new topics such as communication studies, with new patterns of full-time and part-
time courses and with problems of course design per se,
seemed more characteristic of polytechnics, as it is now of
the colleges of education. The universities showed greater
concern than the polytechnics with change in the processes
of teaching, learning and assessment, with small group
work, with new developments in laboratory organization and
new variations on the traditional examination pattern.   In
these respects the colleges share the concerns of the universities.

The enormous choice with which students are now faced on
entry to higher education may be confusing rather than motivating. But a few examples of courses available serve to
show that they offer new opportunities in study and employment, should develop a students' appreciation of relationships between different areas of study, and may include
practical experiences which serve to put theoretical studies
in a broader context and act as a preparation for employment.

In an early interdisciplinary course at a university,
Jevons (1970) designed a BSc degree course to give insight
into the role of science in relation to politics, economics,
industry and philosophy whilst offering a broad covering of
physics with some engineering and computer programming.
Graduates of this course found employment with remarkable
rapidity.   An MSc course was developed subsequently requiring more extended studies of social issues relating to
the sciences.

Numerous other new courses follow this development in
combining studies in social and physical or applied sciences.
One offers a foundation course including behavioural sciences, economics, physical science, mathematics, history
of science and communication studies, prior to study of some
of these subjects in greater depth.   Other courses offer
studies relating to engineering and society or science and
society; another combines science as a mode of knowledge
with communication studies, or chemistry can be combined
with business studies, and so on.   There is, as yet, little

hard evidence that they more effectively motivate students, except in instances where there are high continuing levels of application.

A number of courses in languages now combine studies of language and literature and of social, political and economic institutions in a foreign country or countries, with some time spent in commercial, industrial or educational placements overseas. At the University of Bradford a course of this kind is so competitive that students entering have higher A-level qualifications than do students in any other field of study. An Anglo-French course in European Business Administration has been developed as a joint enterprise of Middlesex Polytechnic and the Management Centre of the École Superieure de Commerce et de l'Administration des Entreprises at Rheims. Half the students on the course are French. Each student spends two years in Britain and two in France, six months of each of these periods being spent in industry (Nuffield Foundation, Newsletter no. 7).

Yet other new degree courses offer librarianship with studies in a language or information science with librarianship. Architecture as a specialist study has been partly replaced by a wide range of design studies, so preparing students for a correspondingly wide range of careers. Theological studies are expanded to comparative study of religions; whilst chemistry is extended to include aspects of physics, geography and biology and is learned through study of a number of unifying themes. There are degrees in dance and education, in creative arts, in home economics, to mention but a few.

It is evident that, if adequate information is supplied and soon enough, no intending student need be denied a choice to suit his preferences.

Other innovatory courses

Epstein (1970) developed a method of teaching biological sciences through discussion of research papers, preferably between undergraduate students and the authors. Discussion of the purposes of research and classification of terms, in response to students' questions, enabled them to gain an extensive vocabulary, sufficient for them to read journals and, in some cases, to attend postgraduate seminars with profit. Courses run in this way led to considerable enthusiasm and advances in understanding. The method has since been used successfully in economics, chemistry and philosophy (Epstein, 1972).

When used at Thames Polytechnic in teaching chemistry, this method raised some problems in finding suitable papers, but with use of small group discussion, it noticeably increased the interest of students in the subject (Nuffield Foundation, Newsletter no. 7, p. 25).

At Bradford University, teachers have found the method useful in developing mature students' understanding of research methods during a first degree course in applied educational studies.

A method of studying intensively in a single field is described by Parlett and King (1971) who introduced 'concentrated study', i.e. full-time study of a single subject for a short period, in this instance physics, at MIT. It provided an opportunity to rethink, from first principles, how the subject should be taught and enabled instruction to be organized in such a way that it permitted close supervision and intellectual contact between instructor and students. This rearrangement of the course gave time for films, lectures by visitors, visits to scientific installations when and where appropriate; the students were expected to work in the library and to look at a variety of texts and original literature.

A course of a different kind, concentrating on development of appropriate skills rather than breadth, is in operation at Sussex University School of Molecular Sciences where students can now take a BSc by thesis. It is commonly known as the Eaborn degree after the chairman of science who introduced it.

CONCLUSION

The foregoing survey of courses devised in universities and colleges shows that developments have been more rapid and exciting than is generally recognized. Nevertheless, we find a high proportion of teachers who are reluctant to be involved in any extensive reorganization of courses which will take up much of their time. In discussion, they comment that, when it comes to consideration for promotion, colleagues who spend all their time on their own research will receive advancement, whereas those who spend time in improving teaching and courses will not receive credit.

It is for this reason, perhaps, that some courses continue

to have examination systems which are at variance with the teachers' objectives, or in which objectives are never made explicit so that students are uncertain what exactly is required of them.

Chapter 5

Who fails or withdraws?

DEFINITIONS AND STATISTICS

The overall impression gained, on reviewing those studies
of student performance which are explicitly concerned with
failure, or which report on differences between those withdrawing and those who succeed in gaining a degree, is of
multifarious and often conflicting evidence. Many different
characteristics and attitudes of students which could be related to their lack of success or their decision to withdraw
have been examined; some of these are seen to be significant in certain departments or among certain groups of students within the institution. However, as we noted in the
previous chapter, institutional contexts vary widely, and
moreover they change over time. In particular, during
the last ten years there has been considerable change in
the curriculum and in course structure, with the genesis of
many new subject areas and combined courses. Students
too have changed, both in their qualifications and preparation for higher education, and in their attitudes towards it.
The search for certain prediction of withdrawal from such
changing situations would be a vain one, and it is not sur-
prising that the evidence is sometimes conflicting.

A further point must be made, however, concerning the
problems involved in interpreting the available evidence.
This is to do with the definitions of withdrawal or failure
used by both the researcher and the administration of an
institution. Official statistics (sometimes called 'wastage
rates' or 'attrition rates') have been collected in most
higher education institutions for the last ten years or so,
and these are often used as the background to, or basis for,
research. A student is recorded as having withdrawn vol-

untarily, or after exam failure; the reason for withdrawal is coded as, say, academic, financial, personal or health.

While such statistics are valuable within the institution to study the differences between departments and their cumulative effect, they are too diverse in origin to be used as a basis for comparison and too concealing to be taken as an adequate account of reasons for withdrawal. A student may be recorded as having withdrawn voluntarily, for example because of parental illness, when in fact he was most unwilling to withdraw and tried very hard to postpone taking the course for a year. One department may assist and encourage those first-year students wishing to change course to do so; another may insist upon them remaining within the chosen course until many see no option but to withdraw, either voluntarily or by failing first-year exams and being required to do so.

In practice, of course, such differences are also found between institutions; thus both departmental and institutional rates will vary widely as a result of official policy and its unofficial implementation, selection procedures, pedagogic and assessment practices, and so on. There will also be gradual change in the composition of an institution's statistics as changes are introduced in such practices. For example, during the 1960s a general trend towards voluntary withdrawal at the expense of failure was noted; it may be surmised that this resulted from less restraint about leaving on the part of students, growing concern about assessment methods which were moderated to include more continuous assessment, a greater respect for the students' decision on the part of some members of staff, and many other similar changes in the 'institutional climate'.

These examples indicate how interlinked are withdrawal statistics and failure statistics, and how they are unlikely to be fully comparable between institutions. Studies examining the similarity of characteristics between withdrawals and failures, and contrasting them with the bulk of students who succeed in gaining a degree in an effort to predict future losses, must be viewed as approximations. They may be examined for trends, patterns and suggested interactions of student with environment rather than for established and certain relationships. The final source of data for an understanding of withdrawal and failure remains the student himself: his own perceptions of the situation and of those aspects which were most influential in his actions and decisions. In a survey of American evidence, Cope (1971) and Tinto (1975) emphasize the primary question of the students' intentions in coming to college. If he did not intend to complete the course in the first place, to class him with other students who have made the decision to withdraw as a result of college experience or who are required to withdraw because of their lack of success is misleading. Although this question may not seem relevant in the British context of competition for university and college places, and hence a highly selected student body, it should be noted that a number of first-year withdrawals from Bradford University said at interview that they had been considering withdrawal for some time before arriving at Bradford.

CHARACTERISTICS OF FIRST-YEAR STUDENTS WHO FAIL

A report by Wilson (1973), part of a large inquiry into the prediction of first-year performance at Aberdeen University, makes a good starting point for the present discussion. Examining one intake of arts and science students on background data and test scores, he found that students passing first-year exams could be distinguished as a group from failing students, although relatively few of the differences between the two groups were statistically significant. Pass students were likely to have slightly higher ratings on neuroticism and motivation and slightly lower ratings on extroversion than fail students; there was virtually no difference between the two groups in scores on a study methods scale. Fail students in arts were more likely to have fathers in manual employment whereas science fail students were more likely to have fathers employed in non-manual occupations. Fail students as a whole seemed to be somewhat weaker academically, in that they were less likely to have obtained two or more 'Higher' passes at the first attempt, more likely to have matriculated in the sixth year at school rather than the fifth, more likely to have poor Certificate passes overall, and more likely not to be aiming at honours degrees (this was especially true of women students failing arts). In addition the headmasters' report was more likely to have expressed reservations about students who subsequently failed, and to have rated them 'not diligent'.

These results are in the directions that would be expected on the basis of previous studies of variables associated with failure and success. However, Wilson stresses the great overlap on any of the measures selected, and that 'even the attempt to combine variables significantly related to fail performance on an individual basis has not successfully distinguished pass students from fails' (p. 26).   Eighteen months after being failed sixty-one of the eighty-five students for whom information was available were continuing with their education at degree level or below.   Twenty of these students had re-entered the university, having sat their exams again after a year's absence; they were not significantly different on any measure from those who failed again at this second sitting, or from those who chose not to resit.

Fail students were asked by questionnaire about the main reason for their difficulties at university.   Three reasons which were frequently mentioned were (i) lack of motivation or not enough hard work, (ii) difficulties with study and in adjusting to teaching, and (iii) wrong choice of subjects or lack of guidance.   Personal problems were also frequently mentioned, particularly by women students.   Some students reacted with equanimity to their failure, having been persuaded to come to university by parents or teachers, or being dissatisfied with what the university had to offer.   A few students felt resentful and cited bad teaching, inadequate guidance and faults in examining as factors contributing to their failure.   The majority blamed themselves for having been badly prepared for their courses or for lacking the ability or will-power to study effectively without guidance and pressure from teachers.   Wilson concludes that 'the case-histories indicate the impossibility of ever attaining a completely accurate prediction of student failure' (p. 32), and points out that although some of the reasons students advance may be considered rationalisations, they indicate the centrality of the student's personal values and perceptions to any explanation of his 'failure'.   It is doubtful in fact whether this emotive institutional interpretation can be applied to students who clearly feel that in accepting the result and leaving university they are not failing but taking a positive step forward.

REASONS FOR TERMINATING STUDIES

More evidence of students' reasons for leaving university courses is given in a large-scale study of students funded by the ILEA (Kendall, 1973).   All students terminating their courses whether voluntarily or not over a period of two

years were subsequently sent questionnaires; just under
half replied.   By far the most common reason given for ter-
mination was 'lack of interest'; 34 per cent of men and 20
per cent of women students (30 per cent overall) giving this
as their main reason, and 69 per cent men and 47 per cent
women giving it as one reason.   Respondents were asked
about their reasons for serious dissatisfaction with their
courses: 20 per cent cited bad course structure, 18 per
cent found their course irrelevant or not as expected, 13 per
cent said that lectures and tutorials were not good enough,
and 12 per cent found their course too theoretical.   While
these observations made after the event conceal diverse attitudes and expectations, and may be viewed as post facto
rationalizations, it is of interest that only 7 per cent expressed serious dissatisfaction because the course was too
difficult.   Thus teachers of many university courses may
err on the side of caution, failing to engage students actively and intellectually.

Of the respondents to this study 8 per cent stated that
their course was too like A-level and lacked depth; as we
mentioned in Chapter 2, this criticism has been encountered
fairly frequently among first-year students at Bradford University.   Altogether three-quarters of Kendall's respondents expressed serious dissatisfaction with their course;
a quarter thought that the supervision and advice they received on academic matters was poor.   Half the students
expressed serious dissatisfaction with their university,
mostly in terms of atmosphere and bad staff-student relations.   Slightly more than a quarter thought the arrangements for advice on personal matters were poor.

An interesting finding of the study concerned the manner
in which courses were discontinued.   Whereas 60 per cent
of the women respondents discontinued study by their own
choice and 34 per cent were refused readmission by their
university, the proportions among men were reversed, 31
per cent terminating by their own choice and 61 per cent
being refused readmission.

THE INVESTIGATION AT BIRMINGHAM UNIVERSITY

The long-term investigations conducted at Birmingham University into the problem of student wastage (Wankowski,
1973) offer further evidence on many of the points so far
mentioned.   In the first year as a whole, the admission

grades of all students withdrawing or failing were found to be
not significantly different from those of students remaining:
however the students withdrawing voluntarily had entered
with significantly higher grades than those failing at the end-
of-year examinations, and the latter were more likely to
have sought help for study difficulties.   In one inquiry,
first-year students defined as academically weak by their
tutors were interviewed and subsequently classed as successful or unsuccessful – required to withdraw.   Analysis
of interview data showed that weak–unsuccessful students
were more likely to admit that they had chosen the wrong
course of study, and tended to report more illness and more
difficulties with specific subjects than did weak–successful
students.   They were also more likely to have been persuaded to enter university (by parents, teachers or friends) and
to have less well-defined goals.   In comparison with weak-
successful students, the weak–unsuccessful students tended
to have higher GCE grades.
    One of the main conclusions from all the Birmingham inves-
tigations was that failure and withdrawal, especially amongst
first-year students, were associated with persuasion to
enter university, study difficulties, lack of interest in the
course, and vagueness about long- and short-range goals;
moreover these aspects were likely to be interrelated.
    Some further explanation of the fourth aspect is required.
All the students in the random sample of a first-year intake
were asked at interview three open-ended questions about
their wishes and intentions in entering higher education.
(It is not clear whether the questions related to vocational
objectives only, or covered other life-goals as well.)   From
the answers to these questions scores for 'intensity of motivation' were derived; the sample was divided into three
groups according to whether the scores indicated that students had very clear, moderately clear, or poorly-defined
goal orientations.   Considerable correlation was found between this measure and success or failure in examinations:
among those with poorly-defined goal orientations 1 in 6
failed and withdrew, whereas among the moderately clear
the proportion was 1 in 16 and among the very clear 1 in 41.
These figures compare with failure rates among poor,
moderate and very high A-level achievers of 1 in 5, 1 in 14
and 1 in 28 respectively.   A clear link was found between
poor motivation defined in this way and study difficulty, in
that 61 per cent of the students attending for educational
counselling had poorly defined goals, whereas only 26 per

cent of a matched group of non-attenders fell into this category. The effect of expressed goal orientation is also clearly seen in the sample of 'weak' first-year students described in the previous paragraph; 45 per cent of the weak-successful students had definite short-range vocational objectives and 59 per cent expressed definite long-range goals, whereas among the weak-unsuccessful students only 17 per cent and 19 per cent respectively expressed definite objectives and goals.

We have already noted, in discussing differences between students, that statistically significant relationships were found between personality (as measured by Eysenck's dimensions of neuroticism-stability and introversion-extroversion) and failure, in a study of the progress of two yearly intakes. The highest failure rate occurred among the neurotic extroverts; 1 in 8 male students in this group failed and withdrew, and 1 in 11 female students. The lowest failure rates were among the stable introvert group, and among stable extrovert women students. Students with study difficulties attending for educational counselling were of a predominantly neurotic disposition. Generally speaking both neuroticism and extroversion contributed to failure; however, that contribution should not be considered in isolation from other factors such as sex and subject of study.

Two further points concerning withdrawal should be mentioned in this context. It seems an important finding that among the random sample of students, who were interviewed periodically throughout their courses, there were no voluntary withdrawals, whereas 3.4 per cent of the other students who sought assistance withdrew voluntarily. Wankowski suggests that this difference may be regarded as a 'Hawthorne effect', participation in the study having had a beneficial influence. The tutors of 110 students who failed and withdrew were asked why they thought this had come about and said that, while twenty-two students were academic casualties, four times that many were known to have other, non-academic reasons contributing to their failure. Wankowski strongly supports the view that 'the prevailing influences in maintaining progress at university have much to do with students' attitudes, wishes, hopes and despairs, frustrations and satisfactions'; all of these will clearly be strongly affected by the students' experiences at university or college.

THE INVESTIGATION AT MANCHESTER UNIVERSITY

A 'before and after' study of withdrawals and failures from
three faculties at Manchester University provides some further insight in this area (Steadman, 1973).   A sample of the
intake answered a questionnaire about home background,
future expectations and opinions of courses early in their
second term.   Students withdrawing were sent a second
questionnaire; 116 returned questionnaires and thirty-five
of these were interviewed, giving what the author describes
as a 'victims' eye-view' of their experience.   Factors
which loomed large in their accounts included misplacement
(with respect to career, course or university), first impres-
sions against the place, disappointment with course content,
failure to form friendships, and friendships formed with
other failures or withdrawers.   Friendships are important
in the early stages in that they enable a student to gauge his
own progress; they lead, however, to the establishment of
patterns of expectations which may influence a student's performance negatively.   Many withdrawers returned home
every weekend, structuring all their social and leisure activities around the home environment and friends there.
Homesickness was prevalent after the first university vacation.   Students felt that immaturity played a large part in
their inability to settle down into university life; however,
Steadman points out that many students who remain at college and succeed are equally immature, and that the important variable may be the initial misplacement of failing students.   In fact 31 per cent of those withdrawing or failing
subsequently joined fresh degree courses and 30 per cent
followed other higher education courses; the proportion of
these failing to finish a second time was small.

FINDINGS OF OTHER INVESTIGATIONS

All the studies that have followed withdrawals to find out
what happened afterwards have uncovered a similar pattern
of recoupment.   Malleson (1967) following up mechanical
engineering students from London colleges, found that two-
thirds had attempted recoupment and two-thirds of these
(i.e. about half the original failed students) had succeeded.
In many cases the courses followed were not in the same
field of study.   In an earlier study of London and Liverpool
students, Kendall (1964) found that two-thirds of the men and

one-third of the women had attempted other degrees, often part-time. Approximately two-thirds succeeded in each case, and many gained further qualifications over and above recoupment, despite the difficulties of doing so while working.

CONCLUSION

These findings again indicate that the majority of students who fail are in no way less capable of gaining a degree. Clearly for some students withdrawal (or failure) is simply an expression of the realization that they are on the wrong course or in the wrong institution; for others it is more a question of the 'wrong time' in the light of personal problems and circumstances. For others still no doubt it is evidence that this was the 'wrong way' - having got off to a bad start they are unable to sort out the mess and establish a better approach. Viewed in terms of the pressures and conflicts of an individual student's life-world - his aims and objectives, his family and relationships, his stage of development and self-image - withdrawal or failure is often a positive adjustment perhaps enabling him to move closer to a decision about what he wants rather than acting in terms of what others expect of him. Or, more negatively, it may be simply a retrieval of some degree of balance, a withdrawal from a situation where the individual feels he has lost control. The 'decompression syndrome', admirably described by Donald Bligh (1977), is still a fairly common experience of new university students, suddenly stranded without the support of standard-bearing parents and teachers.

Chapter 6

Motivation and teaching

In discussing teaching methods that motivate students to work and so to learn more effectively we shall assume that the college environment is at least fairly congenial, that the courses students attend are well planned, and that the recommendations in Chapter 2 concerning new students are followed where necessary.

Even the liveliest teaching can do little to counteract the negative attitudes of a group that has found a course 'irrelevant and boring'. This is most likely to happen where the course plan consists of a list of topics, without reference either to skills students need to acquire in their chosen field or to their interests. For example, courses such as mathematics for chemists, or biochemistry for medical students, are sometimes taught in a way that is congenial to the mathematician or biochemist, but neglects applications to the students' field of study. Ideally teachers who take such courses should be doubly qualified; but where they are not, they should be supplied, or supply themselves, with illustrative examples which the students will find meaningful and useful. Kogut (1975), for instance, has collected an assortment of applications of biochemistry and physiology as used by consultants in hospitals which are suitable for use by pre-clinical teachers.

We have already mentioned, too, the effect of assessment which is at variance with course aims. Students naturally concentrate on what will be assessed and may pay little attention to teachers who expand, however interestingly, on other developments in the field. If a teacher insists that these are important, it seems not unreasonable for students to doubt it, unless its importance is recognized in the course assessment. Otherwise they must conclude that a degree in that subject is given for knowledge and abilities which are out of date or not fully representative of the specialist's needs.

Nor can teaching alone, however stimulating, usually suffice to meet the various needs of new students. The less confident and well prepared need to be involved in initial activities in which they get to know their teachers and fellow students and obtain assistance in overcoming their inadequacies and difficulties. Once they are on the way to improving their knowledge and study methods, and have sufficient information about the aims of the courses they are pursuing and how these will be assessed, they can begin to study relevantly and independently and to profit from the teaching which follows.

Other problems which face the teacher arise from the need to allow for the diversity (considered in Chapters 1 and 3) of students' orientations, levels of maturity, different cognitive and learning styles, and personality traits, in addition to catering for different levels of achievement on entry. Ideally, therefore, teachers need an extensive repertoire of teaching methods to draw from in order to meet the needs of different groups of students. At one extreme they may need to persuade students who were 'spoonfed' at school to take responsibility and to think for themselves, possibly by involving them in group work initially in which the students decide how to tackle a task or problem and jointly prepare a report on their activities (Collier, 1969). At the other extreme they must respond to the diverse interests of students having 'academic', 'political' or 'social intellectual' orientations, who will welcome teaching methods which demand a lot of them but require versatile teachers who can talk to them about different applications or aspects of their subjects, and help them to develop the range of skills needed in pursuing these interests in projects based on empirical work or in writing dissertations. Thus, motivating students demands a knowledge of individuals and their needs in addition to knowledge of teaching methods and of psychologists' findings about motivation.

Studies by psychologists show that the teaching methods most likely to motivate students to learn or to maintain good motivation are those which actively involve them, lead to a sense of achievement, maintain a high level of arousal and, especially in the case of sociable students, provide satisfaction through acceptance by and recognition from a group.

Good teaching methods usually do several or all of these things simultaneously.

STUDENT INVOLVEMENT AND MOTIVATION

It will be appreciated that in the case of adolescent and adult students 'active involvement' does not necessarily imply physical activity or even discussion; it may consist simply in silent thinking on their part. Indeed, whatever students do as part of an activity or experience, it is essential that they should think, reflecting on its implications and what they have learned from it. Any teaching method can be used well or poorly; it is as ineffectual to engage students in an activity of which they do not see the point, or which they find tiresome and needlessly time-consuming, as to lecture at a level above their understanding, or to lecture inaudibly or at a pace which precludes reflection. Needless to say, ineffectual teaching, whether it involves activity or not, has an adverse effect on motivation.

  Like psychologists, students evidently realize the efficacy of activity whilst learning. They are unanimous, for instance, in condemning the practice of dictating notes, contrasting it with methods which allow them to think and to participate. Comments of students at Bradford are typical:

  'When you're writing stuff down at the lecture rate you don't really take in what's being said. In fact you can write something and you won't remember the paragraph ahead, you're just writing, you're not concentrating or listening to it.'

  'I think lectures are more useful if you take your own notes rather than have them dictated; if I read it up and write everything out again I remember more of the lectures than I do in the ones that are dictated and I don't bother to look at again.'

  'You just take lecture notes like a machine really. I think you could probably spend all the evening writing up lecture notes and getting no other work done.'

  'Personally, I like somebody who'll stand up at the front and just lecture, going slowly enough to let us take notes but not put it all on the board. If somebody writes it all on the board, I'll just go to sleep and copy it down; but, if I've got to make my own notes, I stay awake.'

These students know what they need – time to think about the subject under discussion, in whatever way this is provided.   They therefore appreciate teachers who lecture sufficiently slowly for them to compose their own notes, or who duplicate notes in advance so making time available for the class to attempt problems and to discuss difficulties. Thus they say:

'He teaches while you take notes so you understand every thing you put down.'

'Maths is interesting.   You get more involved in lectures and can sit and talk after.   We're given points of the lectures so we don't have to take notes and can work through examples with her which I think is much more interesting. She took degrees in both maths and biology, so she can relate things.'

Indeed, it is hard to reconcile dictation of notes – common as it is – with the conception of a university as pre-eminently a place where students learn to think!   The excuse sometimes given that new students do not know how to take notes cannot justify dictating them, but suggests rather that such students, where they exist, should be assisted in this activity.   For instance, students can be directed to a programmed text such as Rowntree's 'Learn how to study' (1976). Alternatively, some institutions or departments put on courses to assist students in improving study skills including, perhaps, organization of study, reading skills, the making and use of notes, report writing, problem solving and working for examinations.   Lecture notes or pamphlets are produced on each topic; but it is important that students should be engaged in appropriate activities and receive feedback on their performance (Nuffield Foundation Newsletter, no. 5). Some methods of assisting students in these ways have already been outlined in Chapter 2.

Despite many criticisms of lectures by students in the past (Marris, 1964; British Medical Students' Association, 1965; Saunders et al., 1969; Students of Royal Dental Hospital, 1966), first-year students at the University of Bradford make it clear that it is not the method as such but the way it is used which sometimes leads to dissatisfaction.

Nevertheless, there is some evidence that whilst lectures may be as effective as other methods in imparting information, they are rarely as effective, and often less so, in stimulating students to think or to change their attitudes. Bligh (1971) draws this conclusion after assembling the results of nearly two hundred investigations in which lecturing was compared with individual work, group discussion, reading, projects or student-centred teaching. This suggests that it may be important to mix methods not only to meet the different needs of students but also to realize different aims of a course. Where lecturing is the predominant teaching method, it is therefore advisable to allow questioning or discussion, however clear the exposition of subject matter may be.

Another way to involve students, incidentally convincing the less enthusiastic of the value of activity on their part, is to provide early experience outside the classroom. This serves to show that theoretical studies in the university or college represent only a part of the knowledge and qualities required in employment, and sets theoretical studies in a broader context. Even a brief experience of earning a living tends to increase confidence and to lead to greater maturity of outlook. One student at Bradford University who had just entered a sandwich course commented:

'I was in a workshop operating a lathe. I couldn't see the relevance of it while I was there, but I have done since. I met people socially and was living in digs on my own. I think I matured quite a lot and got used to looking after myself.'

We have already seen in Chapter 2 that simply being exposed to a hospital environment, observing staff in action, enabled dental students to learn later theoretical work better than students who received a series of more than twenty lectures in place of this experience (Steubner and Johnson, 1969).

There is some evidence that relevant experience at any time tends to increase motivation and to facilitate subsequent learning. A shift to more favourable attitudes was reported in the case of students of languages at Bradford University after spending a year overseas, especially if they were employed in an industrial or business firm. Students remarked that they had gained in self-confidence and that their perspectives had broadened, whilst research workers who were engaged in evaluating this experience confirmed that the students had become significantly more open-minded (Willis et al., 1977).

In the absence of experience (perhaps because it would take too long), simulation methods may be helpful in the form of role play or case studies. Such methods are currently used in social science and vocational courses including politics, law, management, economics, planning, medi-

cine, nursing and social work. For example, students
studying planning may be given a book of papers relating to
a problem in town planning, comprising correspondence between Local Authority officials and an applicant for a
permit, forms which have to be completed, solicitors' letters written on behalf of the applicant, and notes passed between different officials working for the Authority. These
can be discussed as a case study. Alternatively, members
of the class may play the roles of applicant, officials, etc.,
given only information these persons would have received,
and so to some extent experience the conflicts of interest
involved in arriving at a decision (Taylor, 1971; Walford,
1972; Taylor and Walford, 1978). In either case, involvement is likely to be far higher than it would be if the proce-
dure was simply outlined in a lecture.

Role playing has grown in popularity in training doctors,
nurses and social workers because it can increase insight
into patients' or clients' problems during interactions between them and the expert. One adult student may act the
role of a client or patient who has been a problem to him
whilst another member of the class plays the professional
role. In this way a new approach may be found to deal with
the situation. Discussion amongst the class that has observed the role play contributes further insights into behaviours and alternative ways of looking at the problem.

A brief simulation, or game, may also be used to provoke
discussion. In an entertaining example, a lecturer invited
university teachers to play a game in three groups. Following each round of the game, members of the groups were
streamed by 'attainment' with the result that after ten
minutes or so some teachers found themselves irrevocably
consigned to the bottom streams. They were furiously in-
dignant, interrupting the game to say that its rules were
unfair. At this point the lecturer informed the class that
the real purpose of the game was to introduce a discussion
of the practice of streaming students in schools and colleges.

Another well-established way of involving students and so
enlisting their full commitment and energy is to offer a
choice of topics for projects, dissertations or long essays.
Students commonly remark on the value of such an experience since it provides opportunity to study, in depth, a
topic chosen for its special interest. It also demands
exercise of skill in every stage of the work, in obtaining
information, defining questions or clarifying problems,

setting up hypotheses, finding or developing techniques to make an independent investigation, testing different possibilities in solving problems, synthesizing material from different sources and writing a full report. Students' application and resulting standard of work is often very high. One Open University tutor (Henry, 1977) in discussing the tutorial role when supervizing project work, comments, 'I was amazed at the quality, some were brilliant', adding that several students had had theirs published. Clinical medical students also have published papers on original projects (Wright, 1968). Projects by undergraduate students in universities and colleges of education sometimes earn the laudatory comment from external examiners: 'Master's degree standard.' Interestingly, it is not always students of recognized merit who achieve the best results – hidden talents may be discovered – whilst even should results seem rather disappointing, the learning experiences involved can be valuable.

ACHIEVEMENT AND MOTIVATION

Most comments about teachers and teaching methods reflect in some way the sense of achievement, or its absence, which students experience. One thing they look for is assistance from their teachers in developing their own skills in learning. As one first-year student said of her teachers: 'Some are teaching you as you would teach somebody the alphabet and some are encouraging you to teach yourself.' The latter, of course, requires greater skill and knowledge on the part of the teacher.

   Tutorials and group discussion are often provided in order to help students to understand the subjects they are studying, but as we saw in Chapter 2 may valuably be used to develop skills in note-taking, finding information, writing reports or essays and so on. Indeed, there are many different ways of using group discussion which are outlined by Abercrombie (1970), Beard (1976), Bligh et al. (1975), Ruddock (1978). Students find it helpful to have time set aside to meet a tutor, and the opportunity of going through material until they are sure that they do understand it:
   'Tutorials are a good idea ... if you have a problem it's much easier to say so then. There's a definite meeting time. If other people don't have the same problem the tutor can suggest a time when he's free.'

'... you find out everything from what other people say. Your knowledge builds up and you see where things fit in.'

'You get put on the spot and it's amazing how much you pick up when you're under pressure. When you're actively participating you learn a lot from whatever people have to say; the tutor's just guiding the argument.'

However, unless the tutor uses this method flexibly, problems arise owing to differing needs of members of the group. One of our first-year students could see the problem from two points of view: 'I don't like tutorials much. I think they can be useful, but there tends to be somebody who finds things difficult and the tutor's get to concentrate on them. I sometimes get quite bored. I think there should be tutorials in maths, but that's because I find maths difficult.' In this instance, a skilful tutor might suggest seeing a single student with a difficulty at a different time. If several students share a difficulty, he might divide the group so that he works with those having difficulty, offering other students a problem to solve, or a question to discuss. Of course, this requires that the tutor should have a supply of suitable problems or questions with him.

Other important features of tutorials and group discussion which contribute to a sense of achievement, and so to increased motivation, are the additional information students receive about requirements of their courses and feedback on their own performance. A student's sense of achievement derives from comparing his performance with a standard or, possibly, but not always so usefully, from his ranking relative to other students. If the standards applied by a teacher are never made explicit, students must guess what is required of them. Those who guess wrongly will not have the opportunity of incorporating their teachers' standards. Yet if they are to leave university capable of evaluating their own achievements, they will need to have experience of applying standards in assessing their own and other students' achievements and assessing the relative merits of different systems.

GROUP MEMBERSHIP AND MOTIVATION

The motivating effect of group membership is frequently mentioned in connection with the value of group discussion methods or co-operative ventures such as group projects.

Not only does it keep some students motivated who would idle if left to their own devices but it tends to increase understanding and to arouse enthusiasm. A physics student at Birmingham University engaged in group projects commented: 'I very much enjoyed group studies and felt that I was really sorting something out and learning things' (Black et al., 1968). The Group for Research and Innovation in Higher Education reports on the value of group projects in a number of fields (Nuffield Foundation, Newsletters nos 5, 7). Both staff and students in the electrical engineering department at the University of Salford have found group projects valuable; at Kingston Polytechnic group projects for second-year students studying for an economics degree have aroused considerable enthusiasm; students of business studies at Brighton Polytechnic have shown a great deal of interest in group projects linked to topical issues of local or national importance.

In a medical school, students of biochemistry work in pairs, each pair writing a report on the experiment they perform and presenting this verbally to a group of fellow students and staff. On the social side these laboratory studies prove outstandingly successful; students enjoy them more than traditional courses. Since, in addition, every experiment produces a surprise, or generates a further question, or teaches a technique which will be used in a further study, the level of arousal and sense of achievement must be high (Jepson, 1969).

In any well-planned group work, students develop skills in communication and in personal relationships whilst the group engages in a common task. At the same time, they learn to rely less on authority figures through discussing problems on equal terms with their peers in the group.

LEVEL OF AROUSAL AND MOTIVATION

A feature of some methods which students criticize adversely is that they cause members of the audience to 'switch off'. Dictating notes instead of lecturing, for instance, not only implies that the speaker considers that students cannot be expected to think for themselves - ignoring evidence that they will not learn unless they do - but also tends to be so monotonous that the level of arousal of the audience sinks to a low ebb. Even if the subject and the notes dictated are straightforward, students are apt to forget the content since a high level of arousal is needed for good attention (Lavach, 1973).

Similarly, although the content of a lecture and its preparation may be excellent, a monotonous voice or tempo can lull an audience to sleep. It is therefore important that anyone engaged in speaking should discover whether he is both audible and interesting to listen to. He may do this by taping his lecture, asking an uninhibited colleague to listen to it and comment or, possibly, by using a questionnaire inviting students to make comments. If he seems to need expert help some universities now have University Teaching Methods Units whose staff may be qualified to assist him; or co-operation can sometimes be obtained from lecturers in colleges of education or schools of drama who specialize in training students to speak effectively. Advice can also be found in books: Chapter 2 of 'Improving teaching in higher education' (University of London Teaching Methods Unit, 1976) includes advice written to assist new lecturers in preparing and delivering a short lecture at a course for new lecturers. If a teacher has an incurably dull voice, he need not despair; but he must work harder to use emphasis and pauses to make his delivery more easily comprehensible. He can also vary the presentation by using interesting illustrations, whether visual or verbal, or by allowing some time for questions and answers, or a 'buzz' session in which members of the audience are invited briefly to discuss a question. When he resumes, using some of their answers arousal tends to increase again. Or in the event that the lecturers' voice is weak, and the audience large, an obvious solution is to use a microphone. In these ways attention and motivation can be maintained.

Other ways of increasing arousal, and consequently motivation, are by enthusiastic teaching, by provoking curiosity through questioning or referring to current research and problems which have been found difficult to solve, or through competitive 'games' designed to improve learning. It is worth remembering, too, that a learner is most likely to return to incomplete activities, whereas completed tasks tend to be more quickly put out of mind.

Even a student who is not very interested in study will respond to teaching methods which are stimulating, to teachers who are enthusiastic and to techniques that involve interesting or competitive activities such as simulation or games. A game for undergraduates in civil engineering has been developed at Heriot Watt University (Cowan and

Morton, 1973) to improve the players' ability to identify forces in the members of pin-jointed trusses.   This has resulted in improved appreciation of structural behaviour. An 'information game' used in teaching biochemistry in which students work in groups of seven, each participant being given only part of the findings in a case of metabolic disease, has proved popular and successful with pre-clinical medical students (Smith and Jepson, 1972).   Suggestions for other games may be found in Taylor (1971), Walford (1972) and Taylor and Walford (1978).

CLASSROOM INTERACTIONS AND MOTIVATION

Interactions in the classroom, whether in schools or colleges, have been too little explored to take the important place they deserve in a chapter on teaching methods.   A number of studies surveyed by Rosenshine (1971) suggest that some five characteristics of teachers may be particularly favourable in promoting motivation and achievements amongst their pupils or students.   These are (i) good structure in teaching which enables the students to follow easily, (ii) a diversity of cognitive styles allowing the teacher to express or illustrate ideas in ways which appeal to different students, and to provide a richness and variety of classroom experiences, (iii) use of students' contributions, possibly because this tends to increase their involvement, (iv) enthusiasm, and (v) warmth, shown in friendliness and appreciation of the students' efforts.   Further research is needed to determine how far these and other characteristics of teachers influence students' performance.
   The effect of verbal teaching style on attainment of educational objectives in physics has been investigated in a longitudinal study by Houston and Pilliner (1974) with older pupils in schools.   Study of interactions in the classroom showed that teaching styles ranged from authoritarian and dogmatic to 'open-ended'.   Authoritarian teachers tended to interact with the class in an expository way, rarely asking questions and only seldom involving students' participation.   At the other end of the spectrum were teachers who were skilled exponents of the open-ended style, providing situations for their pupils based on experiments and expecting pupils to draw their own conclusions based on their own interpretation of results.   They constantly asked questions and prompted pupils to make their own discoveries.   Thus,

at one extreme, teachers tended to think for their pupils, at the other they provoked the pupils into thinking for themselves.   Interestingly it was the second kind of teacher who proved significantly more successful, not only in enabling pupils to develop more complex kinds of thinking but even in simple comprehension questions and recall of information. On the whole too, the 'open-ended' style was the most successful in developing favourable attitudes towards physics. A consequence of the traditional type of course which some pupils were studying was that overall they all lost interest and knew less about the social and general implications of the subject than did pupils whose courses were more 'open-ended'; however, they learned to be as objective in making scientific judgments.

Hornsby-Smith (1973) suggests that the prevalence of expository styles of teaching in physical sciences in higher education results in unfavourable attitudes.   He recommends a move to more heuristic teaching styles.   Like the Nuffield Science programmes in schools, and use of 'open-ended' experiments in some laboratory courses in higher education, these require that students should think through problems for themselves, deciding on their own experiments and requesting help from teachers or demonstrators only when they cannot proceed unaided.   The role of the teacher is to assist, not by telling students what to do, but by eliciting new lines of thought through questioning and discussion.   As we shall see in Chapter 7, good teachers also use assessment of students' course work to help them to progress to more advanced ways of thinking and levels of understanding and to more skilful forms of expression and inquiry.

Motivation and assessment

However true it may be – as some students and teachers assert – that traditional forms of assessment by examination have detrimental effects on learning and teaching, there can be no doubt that assessment is motivating in some ways. Almost all students wish to obtain a qualification and are willing to work for it in any way that is required of them. In addition, students often say that tests and course requirements provide an incentive to work, obliging them to reorganize and reappraise what they learned in studying topics which initially they did not see as related. It is assessment of this kind, usually at the end of a term or session, involving teachers in a judgmental role, which is most criticized for its alleged effects on relationships between teachers and students. In contrast, assessment of course work which is designed to help students continuously to improve their performance is valued by almost all students, for this enables them to develop skills and abilities in learning and gradually to incorporate the standards of experts in their chosen field of study. Whilst this, too, involves the teacher in judging students' achievements, he may do so informally in his role as adviser, whether in discussion with the student or in writing comments on his work. It is possible also to have work discussed by a group of students with the teacher as leader or participant, all members of the group offering constructive criticisms and suggestions for improvement. In these ways the teaching role largely replaces the judgmental role of the examiner.

It may be helpful to think of assessment as having two main purposes. The first determines which students qualify to proceed to further courses or to be awarded degrees which give entry to a variety of professions and other intellectually demanding occupations. The second offers information to students about work they have undertaken in a way that enables them continuously to improve their performance. To use an industrial analogy, these fulfil respectively the inspection and the production functions. During the last fifteen years or so there has been a steady shift in emphasis from the first to the second. But whereas in industry there is usually sufficient expertise in controlling the production function to guarantee a sound product, in education the greater number of variables involved – and the imperfect state of our knowledge of processes in learning – combine to make the outcome considerably less certain. Further research into learning and teaching processes is needed. In addition, the autonomy of the educational 'raw material' has no parallel in industry; students themselves to a large extent determine the outcome of the processes in which they are involved.

QUALIFICATIONS AND MOTIVATION

The function of higher education in providing qualifications is an important one motivationally. When in the late 1960s some students began to demand that examinations, or even all assessment, should be abolished, it became apparent in discussion that this would lead to a proliferation of qualifying examinations for the professions. It was evident, too, that the demand for abolition of examinations came mainly from a minority of students, who were predominantly in social science departments, whereas students pursuing vocational and science courses were on the whole well content with the examination system, welcoming the incentives and evidence of achievement which a classified degree system offered. Teachers and students pointed also to dangers in abolishing assessment. If there were no degree classes to refer to, the opinions of teachers would carry far more weight than formerly when giving references for their students, and some university teachers might devote considerable time to setting and marking examinations for entry to the professions. Indeed, proliferation of entry examinations to professions seemed highly probable if there were no first degree examination results from which to estimate students' intellectual performance. Even students who wished examinations to be abolished agreed that in the interests of public safety intending doctors and engineers

would need to show evidence of competence. Thus, on reflection, it seemed that the classified degree system offered
an economical way of providing information to potential employers or to members of the public, in addition to having a
motivating effect for the majority of students.

THE PURPOSES OF EXAMINATIONS

This is not to say, however, that every kind of assessment
has a beneficial effect on students' motivation or performance. If a course and its assessment have not been carefully planned, motivation from the assessment system may be
at variance with that which teachers intend. This can sometimes account for teachers' disappointment with students who
seem motivated solely 'to work for examinations' and who
find their teachers' enthusiasms for new developments in
their field merely distracting. Study of the course and
assessment system may show that the latter consists mainly
in examinations requiring primarily a good memory for lecture notes and standard texts; there is no paper, or project,
allowing students to gain credit for understanding new developments, for critical evaluation of articles and research
papers, or for evidence of capacity to study in depth. In
fact, the examination questions may never require levels of
thinking higher than those involved in presenting memorized
material in a well-organized and clear fashion. Yet
teachers would say that their aims far exceeded this.
    Limitations of this kind in some examinations became
apparent during investigations in the 1960s. In 1968, Black
reported results of an analysis of physics final degree examinations, concluding that most papers were of a common pattern, which enabled candidates to gain high marks through a
well-organized memory, and that questions were neither
systematic nor searching.
    Beard and Pole (1971) in an investigation into the content
of biochemistry examinations set in 1968 confirmed Black's
finding that teachers tended to set questions requiring little
more than recall of information.
    Since the results of finals are used in selecting students
for postgraduate studies, this could be unfortunate. Students having well-stocked memories do not necessarily make
good research workers. In a geography department at Newcastle, Whiteland (1966) found that whilst outstanding examination candidates usually managed to write competent

theses, less than half of the undergraduates whose thesis gained A marks, obtained examination marks as high as B+. This bears out the claim, made by psychologists and students, that creative individuals are not necessarily good examinees. Hudson (1966) found that a third of Fellows of the Royal Society had gained a second or worse at some time during their university careers, probably because the examination system did not motivate them to do their best.

Limitations of this kind are avoided by teachers who prepare courses based on specification of carefully considered aims and objectives, relating these with teaching methods and assessment from the beginning. For instance, Ross (1972-7) has written an entire course in postgraduate law in this way, specifying for each topic an objective or objectives, planned student experience/activity, materials/equipment to be prepared/available, and methods of evaluation. Thus students are constantly assessed in a manner appropriate to the activity: e.g. in studying probate and wills, they may be required to list possible ways of dividing up an estate, to predict their effects, to select the most appropriate in view of the testator's wishes, the type and value of the benefit conferred, the burden of duty, cost of administering the estate, suitability of the executors and the extent of their control of the estate. In group discussion of students' responses, instructors note how well they have grasped the principles. By the time final examinations are reached they have already practised the various activities required of them in their profession and have a book to revise from in which each activity has been carefully analysed, together with a record of their own corrected responses and any problems raised. There is no doubt that they have practised and gained some measure of skill in every relevant activity. This motivates students by amply satisfying their desire to know what the course is about, and by supplying feedback as to their success in activities and exercises.

Even a considerably less detailed analysis of course aims may lead to diversification of forms of assessment. For instance, in an English department, Brockbank (1969) and his colleagues chose to employ six different kinds of assessment for their students. Similarly, the Australian College of General Practitioners prepared a variety of theoretical and practical tests for general doctors wishing to become members of the College (Beard, 1969b) including skills in interviewing and examination of patients, diagnosis and treatment, in addition to knowledge relating to medical subjects.

In diversifying assessment to cover specified abilities, teachers are a stage nearer to providing students with a fuller description of what constitutes competence in the subject they teach and to being able to diagnose and remedy students' weaknesses. Examinees have a clearer understanding of what is required of them and so are better able to prepare themselves. If students' main interest is in preparing for examinations, or other forms of assessment, they will as a consequence develop an expertise in a full range of activities representing competence – and conceivably excellence – in their field.

Careful consideration of course requirements may also result in developing new forms of examination. At the University of Edinburgh, Miller and Parlett (1974) assisted colleagues in a science department to devise a paper to measure understanding of scientific principles underlying the first three years of an undergraduate course. Initially, a paper was prepared containing sixteen short questions and two long ones, but in the second year twenty short questions only were set, to be completed in the usual three hours. Teachers felt that this kind of question constituted a better test of the thinking process. It is of interest, therefore, that although a practice paper was supplied to students, some who were deemed first class by their teachers showed serious gaps in understanding. This raises questions concerning three-hour papers with many options. It is sometimes said that these enable students to prevent their inadequacies being detected. Perhaps some teachers need to analyse further what a first-class performance entails in order to ensure that this is what is assessed.

Various other examining methods have been devised specifically to test students' ability to think. Students may be asked to comment critically on the argument in a quoted passage or short article and to discuss further the questions under consideration. Science students may be invited to comment on real or purported experimental results, explaining what they are about and accounting for all the results recorded. In one medical biochemistry department, students are asked in addition to 'Give some brief theoretical background against which the problem and your solution can be set. Indicate what further investigations would help test the correctness of your explanation' (Beard and Pole,

1971). Helfer and Slater (1971) describe a method of presenting diagnostic problems in a deck of ninety-six consecu-
tively numbered cards and containing a specific historical
fact concerning a patient, a given physical finding, or a
single laboratory result. This method, they say, has the
capability of selecting out students who may require special
assistance in developing skills in clinical problem solving.
Thus it combines assessment and teaching functions as most
good assessment methods do. Perhaps this is why students
have received it enthusiastically.

Writing answers to old examination papers is one time-
honoured method of revising. What students learn thereby
may be too narrowly circumscribed unless the purposes and
content of each paper, and of the entire course and assessment system are reconsidered from time to time. Any sug-
gestion that all examining might be achieved by one method,
for instance by multiple-choice tests (Young and Gillespie,
1972) seems out of touch with the teaching aspect of examinations and assessment. Just conceivably, of course, this
method may be so adaptable that it is capable of being developed to assess a very wide range of abilities and skills.
If this proves possible, then the reliability of multiple-
choice tests, their suitability for marking by computer and
the possibility of accumulating 'banks' of questions from
which future tests can be drawn, will make this an attrac-
tive alternative to methods requiring considerable marking
time. However, it is doubtful whether multiple-choice
tests can be used to teach or test ability to write, say, a
critical account of events or to develop an argument, any
more than an essay paper can normally be used to test
ability to analyze and to evaluate previously unseen information or to solve new problems.

THE RELIABILITY OF EXAMINERS

Multiple-choice tests at least have the advantage of high, or
even perfect, reliability on the part of persons or computers
marking them. A perennial problem in marking essays and
course work is that teachers' opinions differ concerning the
standard of work. Such factors as students' handwriting
(Kandel, 1936), the number of papers already marked (Farrell and Gilbert, 1960), errors which examiners take note of
(Natkin and Gould, 1967), or the candidates' volubility in
oral exams (Evans et al., 1966), may all appreciably influence the marks given.

Despite belief in many university departments that standards of different members of staff closely agree, this may
be achieved more than teachers realize by their previous
discussion of students which develops similar expectations
in them all. In engineering where close agreement seems a
reasonable expectation, McVey (1975) found that it tended to
be high only under the normal circumstances in which students' performance was discussed and marks were left on
papers when seen by a second examiner. In an experiment
in which names of candidates were deleted and marks were
given quite independently by pairs of examiners, the greatest difference on any one paper rose to 28 per cent, although it was no more than 10 per cent before these precau-
tions were taken.

Other surveys of investigations into agreement between
examiners confirm that it is less than teachers commonly
believe and, on occasion is no better than would occur by
chance (Beard, 1969a, 1976; Cox, 1967). There is some
evidence that more reliable results are obtained in marking
essays if questions are graded into a few categories, e.g.
five, say A to E, rather than by giving numerical marks.
Possibly the former system allows examiners to exercise
their judgment more flexibly. If a fifteen-point scale is
used, e.g. A+ to E-, then assigning answers to one of five
piles, which are subsequently graded more finely, helps to
keep examiners' standards fairly constant.

Students are aware of the unreliability of marking essays
and have written about it (Saunders et al., 1969). There
is no doubt that uncertainty concerning fairness in marking
contributed to students' concern that examinations should be
abolished. They argued that a series of marks obtained
over a period of time was likely to give a fairer estimate of
a student's abilities.

It may also be helpful to list headings under which essay
questions, reports or projects will be considered. This
not only contributes to greater agreement between assessments by different examiners but serves to inform students
as to what will be looked for; and this, as we have seen, is
important in contributing to motivation and to success. For
instance, headings suggested for marking mathematical projects at Southampton (Hirst and Biggs, 1969) included: exposition (mathematical accuracy, clarity, literary presentation); study of literature (understanding, relating different
sources, finding new sources); originality (examples cited,
examples constructed, new treatments and proofs of stan-

dard results, simple generalizations, original researches); and scope of topic (conceptual difficulty, technical difficulty, relationships with previous studies, relevance of material included, coverage of the topic). Some guidance of this kind is desirable in all forms of continuous assessment, except perhaps in the case of continuous tests. However, it can become restricting if stated percentages of marks are assigned to each category.

CONTINUOUS ASSESSMENT AND MOTIVATION

As students pointed out in the late 1960s (Saunders et al., 1969) continuous assessment met many of their criticisms of end-of-year examinations. Judgment of a student's work was based on a number of samples, instead of a single paper or exercise, so making for greater reliability; there was time for improvement as a result of discussion and experience, enabling the student to impress his teachers more favourably if he was ill-prepared initially, and anxiety tended to be less when marks towards the final assessment could be accumulated gradually, instead of being concentrated in a few days or weeks when, for some reason, a student might not perform at his best.

Experience of continuous assessment has tended to modify enthusiasm for it; assessment of every piece of work is usually found inhibiting since students feel that they cannot afford to experiment, whilst the work-load entailed for students in preparing assignments, and for staff in marking them, may prove prohibitive. For these reasons intermittent assessment has usually been preferred; students perhaps present their three best essays, or alternate or occasional pieces of work, for final assessment. Even this has not satisfied some critics. Teachers sometimes regret having to take account of first- or second-year marks for a student who has improved greatly subsequently; they would like to rate him first class if that is what he has become. Students who do not work hard throughout a course but have ability to excel may be similarly handicapped. This raises the whole question of what students should be doing with their time: should they always be preparing assignments, or should there be time to think and to mature or to use in developing wider interests?

At Bradford University first-year engineering and science students who have been assessed by frequent tests and other

course work have reacted in a number of different ways
saying variously:

'I like the idea of assessment by tests and essays, but
you've got to accept the fact that it is hard work. It is
continual pressure....'

'It's a lot easier to work gently all through the year than
to make a mad rush just before exams.'

'It is a bit difficult really because you want to do extra
work like background reading but you must use the time to
revise for tests.'

'I don't mind continuous assessment for practicals but
I'd prefer a major exam on theory. I think it /contin-
uous assessment/ is more strain.'

'It's definitely made me work harder than I ever did at
school.'

It is clear, therefore, that there is something to be said
on both sides and that students differ in their reactions to
different kinds of assessment. Highly anxious and less
mature students, or extroverts who need constant pressure,
may benefit from intermittent assessment. Less anxious
and more independent, self-directed students, or introverts, may prefer assessment by yearly examinations. On
the other hand, mature students of education usually say
that intermittent assessment of course work suits them
better, since they cannot do justice to important subjects in
short essay answers in examination papers; they want time
to study subjects in depth and to write extended essays or
reports on their findings.

MARKING AND MOTIVATION

Although they are undeniably forms of assessment, marking
and discussion of students' work can be among the most in-
structive methods of teaching. The essence of using written comments, or tutorials, to motivate students to do
better, is to involve them in appraisal of their own work so
that they appreciate its errors and limitations but also see
new possibilities. Some kinds of reactions by teachers
make such a development unlikely. Assignment of grades
without comment is one such response, for this not only

fails to involve the student but leaves him uninformed as to what he might do differently. He can change his approach next time, hoping for improvement, but may end completely exasperated, like the science student who said:

'I've found that if you do work hard and give in a good essay you get the same mark. It satisfies me more to write a good essay, but you know you get 7 whatever you give in. If you copy out of a text-book you get 7, or if you work hard, put in a lot of reading and express it in your own words, you still get 7. I've decided that it's not worth it.'

Evidently the initial motivation of this student was being rapidly dissipated by an uninformative teacher. Presumably the standards of the teacher and student differed in some way. But what could be the standards of a teacher who was indifferent as to whether a written answer was copied from a text-book or based on extensive reading? And how could he interpret his role as a teacher to include so little communication?

Yet this teacher is not alone in being too uncommunicative. The Open University has found it essential to assist the academics it recruits as part-time tutors to teach by correspondence. It does this partly by conducting local assignment marking exercises and discussions between new and experienced tutors, and partly by providing written guidance for tutors (Grugeon, ed., 1973; Sewart, ed., 1977). The authors of the earlier document are critical not only of grades without comments but also of what they term 'closed comments', e.g. 'This just won't do.', 'Style.', 'Disorganized and inchoate', or 'Your spelling is atrocious.'. Although these are comments they cannot be said to have communicated anything more than irritation; they fail to involve the students in making efforts to improve, to think more effectively, to consider new models or to set higher standards. Such comments discourage effort, diminishing the will to improve and impeding full understanding of what went wrong. Open University tutors are therefore advised to develop a more tentative style of comment, preceding specific criticisms, since this is more likely to encourage students to improve written performance and to extend their thinking. For instance, 'It is sometimes difficult to distinguish between that given and that proved, isn't it? For example ...'.

Comments made by different tutors to the same errors are also contrasted in examples from a variety of subjects (pp. 42-57), for example:

(i) Quite a good assignment although you do not understand texts 12 and 13.

(ii) It would be in your interest to look again at texts 12
and 13.

(iii) You have given some good answers but sometimes
come up against obstacles, e.g. questions 2 and 10
(see comments on paper). You would do well to
read text 12, page 17 and text 13, page 13.

(i) and (ii) suffer in that references are unspecific and a
lack of sympathy is evident: the student may well have
read the text three or four times. The first comment (i)
while being mildly encouraging does not offset the unsympathetic nature of the second remark. (ii) is completely
impersonal and unsympathetic. Both (i) and (ii) would
probably discourage a student and even lead to distress
on his part. In neither case does it appear that the student would be induced to study closely the comments made
in the script. (iii) is encouraging and should enhance the
motivation of the student. It is conceivable that the student would be motivated sufficiently to read and study the
comments on the script. The identification of particular
areas in scripts is valuable educationally; the student
should not be daunted by the prospect of reading two
pages only....

Clearly it would be valuable for all new teachers in
higher education (and many more experienced ones) to read
this text, for they too can influence student's motivation by
the nature of the comments they make on their work. Those
who do this well may receive glowing tributes, such as: 'I
so look forward to getting my work back - it's like getting a
particularly challenging and interesting letter from a friend'
(Rogers, 1977).

Ideally methods of marking are discussed by all teachers
in a school, or department. Where this is done, most
teachers agree that it is good tactics to find something to
praise initially, only later drawing attention to inaccuracies
in spelling and sentence construction, etc., indicating
errors of fact and misunderstandings, pointing to need for
explanation or for additional references, or helping a student to see why an answer, or part of one, lacks relevance
or appropriateness. In some cases, a system of letters in
the margin, corresponding with underlinings in the text,
suffices to draw attention, say, to incorrect spelling (it may
be most helpful to write the word correctly), or errors in
English, whilst longer comments are reserved for errors in
argument, misunderstanding, irrelevance, and so on.

PEER-ASSESSMENT AND SELF-ASSESSMENT

A method increasingly in use to help students to incorporate the standards of experts is to involve them from an early stage in assessing their own work and that of peers. This happens, for instance, in some schools of architecture where students of different years come together in 'juries', led by a tutor, to discuss designs prepared by members of the group. Views at all levels of sophistication may be expressed, but over a period of time students tend to acquire the more mature standards. Similarly group discussion of students' essays, book reviews, or work proceeding in a group project should have a beneficial effect on students' capacity to judge the quality of work and so to raise their own standards.

Rating scales for peer- and self-assessment are a newer development which, at first sight, seem less educationally valuable than discussion. Medical students are invited to rate each other, and themselves (say from 1 to 4), on a number of attributes, e.g. fund of knowledge, conscientiousness, leadership, appearance, clinical judgment, doctor-patient relationship, team spirit, interpersonal relationships, intellectual curiosity, technical ability, potential as a physician, integrity, ability to communicate; and their peers only for desirability as a partner, desirability as a consultant and desirability as your own physician (Linn et al., 1975).

This scale has proved highly reliable over a short period of time, and has proved interesting in that students consistently rated themselves lower than they were rated by their peers. Morton and Macbeth (1977) confirm this tendency. Possibly the value of such scales, and the exercise of self-rating, is to draw attention to qualities that are considered desirable in a physician and so to increase students' motivation to achieve them. Similar scales can be devised for other courses (Barke, 1969; Kennel et al., 1973), but there seems little scope for their use by students of the majority of undergraduate subjects.

STUDENTS' ASSESSMENT OF COURSES AND TEACHING

Assessment by students of courses and teaching is normally more useful to teachers who wish for information than to the students themselves. Conditions which make students eager

to assess a course or their teachers are normally unsatis-
factory in some way: the course is too difficult, too con-
densed or repeats too much of what students have already
studied; teachers give too little feedback on performance,
talk too fast, or offer insufficient information as to the way
in which their subjects will develop and how students will be
assessed, etc. (Flood-Page, 1974).   On the other hand, if
all is well on the whole, students may feel that yet another
questionnaire given out by a member of staff is merely a
nuisance and so fail to fill it in.   Since this is frustrating
to the member of staff who genuinely wants information, it
may be better instead, or in addition, to hold a departmental meeting in which the course is discussed and teaching
can be mentioned incidentally.   Motivation for attendance
can be supplied by making the occasion a social one.

There is a difficulty, of course, if a member, or members, of the teaching staff are reluctant or unwilling to
accept comments from students.   Students may then feel
motivated to say a great deal but, perhaps, recognize that
it will be useless to do so.   Thus, like moderate satisfaction with a course, intense dissatisfaction can result in
silence or poor response.   A meeting with an approachable
course tutor who will act as intermediary is a possible solution.   Otherwise the course and its teachers will be
'assessed' by the students through withdrawal, absence and
apathy.   Teachers may then comment that 'the students are
not motivated', unaware of how far their own attitudes have
contributed to this state of affairs.

Chapter 8

Can we select successful students?

The extent and variety of problems in predicting which students will succeed in higher education does not seem to have been appreciated, perhaps because the greater part of research into the subject was not reported until the beginning of this decade. Recent major studies have been made at Lancaster by Entwistle, Nisbet, Entwistle and Cowell (1971), Entwistle and Brennan (1971), Entwistle (1972) and at the National Foundation for Educational Research, under the direction of Choppin (1972, 1973, 1976). At Birmingham University, Wankowski has made a more general and long-term study of students and their problems in which indicators of success and failure have been explored incidentally. In Scotland, Powell (1973) has made an extensive study relating entry qualifications with success in degree courses.

Since decisions to accept students into higher education are made largely on the basis of A-level grades, their value as predictors of success has been investigated over a period of time. In early studies, correlations with degree classes between variables such as grades at A-level, head teachers' predictions, teachers' predicted grades and number of O-levels, were mostly between 0.1 and 0.4 and were typically around 0.2 (Petch, 1961, 1963; Himmelweit, 1963; Bagg, 1970; Choppin and Farr, 1972; Christie and Mills, 1973). Despite these rather poor relationships, the authors concluded that A-level results were the best predictors available and that, when taken into consideration together with other variables such as school reports and O-level results, they contributed more than other variables to the multiple prediction.

A-LEVEL GRADES AND DEGREE PERFORMANCE

As we shall see, there are a number of reasons why this is unhelpful in particular cases. In the first place, consideration of a few extreme instances will serve to show how misleading correlations with A-level results may be. Let us suppose, for example, that in a department able to insist on 'high standards', students are accepted only if they achieve three As in A-level examinations - then since their performance initially is identical it cannot serve to predict differences between them at the end of the course; the correlation between their A-level grades and degree results will be indeterminate. This will be equally true even should they all gain first-class degrees! The department, and the institution to which it belonged, would doubtless feel that they had done well to select in this way; nevertheless, until it is shown that students progressively less well qualified perform progressively worse there can be no evidence as to the predictive value of A-levels. Indeed wherever the intake is limited with respect to A-level grades, for instance to C or above, the corresponding correlation between A-level and degree grades is likely to be near zero since students who are so nearly equal on entry are quite likely to change places in the classified degree results.

A different reason for low correlations between A-level results and degree classes is that students may enter a university or college course to study a speciality which is new to them, or in which their A-level studies are not particularly relevant. Thus a student having A-levels in, say, English, geography and art may be accepted into a sociology department. Since there are fewer established sixth-form courses in sociology, the subject may be introduced ab initio at university or college. Thus, performance at school may be of little consequence except in so far as it indicates interest in and ability for academic study. If a student finds the new course more motivating, although she was formerly poor she may come to excel.

The case of an entrant to an engineering course may be quite different. He will almost certainly require a good knowledge of mathematics and either physics or chemistry, because the university of college course builds on these. The hierarchical nature of the science subjects make it a considerable handicap to a student entering higher education without one of the subjects normally required, or having poor command of the subjects he has studied. How-

ever, we should note that it is the initial requirements
which make for difficulty. If an alternative course were
provided which would enable these students to catch up and
to acquire the essentials of new subjects, they might do as
well as the better qualified.

In addition to these common reasons for poor correlation
with, and poor prediction from, A-level results there are
numerous other variables which may affect individual students or groups of students: preparation at school may have
ranged from expert coaching to inexpert teaching by a tem-
porary teacher or someone unqualified in the subject; some
students develop late, teaching methods and teachers' per-
sonalities may be more or less congenial at university or
college than at school, a student may put behind him ham-
pering problems at home or acquire new problems in his
personal life in college, a student's involvement in social
activities may increase with opportunity, or owing to boredom with academic work due to excessive revision, and so
on. Such factors should be borne in mind when attempting
to interpret correlations found in major studies at the beginning of the chapter. Nor should we neglect the evidence
which follows concerning effects of personality on consis-
tency of results.

In the NFER study, correlations of mean A-level grades
with degree performance in English universities and colleges varied between 0.19 in arts faculties to 0.42 in engineering, giving a mean correlation overall of 0.28 (Choppin et al., 1972, 1973, 1976). In Scotland, rather higher
overall correlations were obtained having a median value of
0.39 from a comparable mean grade variable (Powell, 1973).

Selection from table 9.4 in 'Degrees of excellence' by
Entwistle and Wilson (1977) shows differences between subjects obtained in the Rowntree project. Whilst most of
these correlations are significant, at least at the 0.05
level, i.e. one would expect to obtain such large correlations in less than one in twenty comparable samples if there
was no relationship, it is evident that the most useful predictor would be first-year marks - if only these were available. Since measures of motivation, study methods and
hours studied are not very reliable, A-level grades seem to
be the best initial predictor, poor as they are as indicators
of success in arts, humanities and social science subjects.

Contingency tables showing number of students gaining
particular A-level grades and degree results in recent
studies will serve to show more clearly what such findings
imply.

TABLE 1 Correlations of predictive measures with degree results, by area of study

Selected variables	Languages		Humanities		Social sciences		Pure sciences		Applied sciences		Mathematics	
	Year 1	3	Year 1	3	Year 1	3	Year 1	3	Year 1	3	Year 1	3
1st-year marks	0.39		0.57		0.34		0.53		0.74		0.71	
No. of O-levels	0.16		0.07		0.08		0.10		0.19		0.22	
A-level grades	0.16		0.19		0.11		0.29		0.53		0.49	
Motivation	0.16	0.15	0.23	0.09	0.15	0.24	0.16	0.30	0.22	0.39	0.35	0.26
Study methods	0.17	0.20	0.26	0.29	0.09	0.18	0.23	0.35	0.31	0.28	0.18	0.39
Hours studied	0.13	0.17	0.31	0.33	0.14	0.16	0.17	0.21	0.38	0.16	0.24	0.21
Statistical significance p 0.05 if r	0.13		0.18		0.12		0.11		0.25		0.19	

From N. Entwistle and J. Wilson (1977), table 9.4.

Two contrasting studies of marks obtained in studies of physics students are of particular interest.

King (1973), in an investigation at Newcastle assigned points to grades obtained in the three best A-level examination results (A = 5 ... E = 1) and correlated these with degree results in physics for 185 students. The resulting correlation of 0.39 is quite high. Table 2 shows numbers of students in each category.

TABLE 2

| A-level points | Degree class | | | | |
	I or II$_1$	II$_2$	III	Pass	Fail
12 or more	40	30	20	10	0
11	20	30	25	18	7
9 or 10	6	25	33	24	12
less than 9 (mostly 8)	9	17	35	22	17

A contrasting result obtained for a number of universities is that of Elton (1968) who obtained results for physics students from nine institutions: two colleges of London University, an institute with recognized teachers of London University, two large civic universities, a university which was a university college in the 1950s, two colleges of the University of Wales and one new technological university. Students' A-level results on entry proved to be substantially in agreement with what might be described as the 'pecking order' of the institutions concerned.   Nevertheless drop-out overall was 20 per cent, varying between 9.6 and 38.0 per cent; the better the entry, the higher were the qualifications of those who failed to stay the course. Thus, there was little predictive value in the A-level grades as far as drop-out was concerned.   Moreover, although a student having an A in physics at entry was certainly more likely to get some sort of degree than one having a lower grade, those having a grade E in A-levels did not perform substantially worse than those with higher grades, up to and including B.   Three colleges having identical qualifications in students at entrance passed 42, 38 and 72 per cent of their intake with honours.

Elton concludes that the attainment of students at a university may depend almost as much on the idiosyncracy of the university as on the students' abilities.

It is evident from Elton's findings and even from King's contingency table that the cut-off points normally chosen for university selection must lead to exclusion of many students who would be capable of getting degrees and possibly even good degrees. Elton's is one investigation which included students having poor qualifications at entry. A study involving sixty students of education, who would normally have taken non-degree courses but who were allowed to share a university course for first-year honours students at the New University of Ulster, is reported by G.A. Brown (1971). He found that the student teachers had lower failure rates than the students accepted for the university course although they included fewer higher-scoring candidates. He therefore concluded that a wider range of students than had hitherto been considered could successfully study university courses. However, all of these students on entry had some A-level results and, whereas two-thirds of those having three Ds, or an equivalent (i.e. 6 points on King's scale) transferred to degrees, only 23 per cent of students having 2 Es (i.e. 2 points) were allowed to do so. As might be expected from the earlier discussion in this chapter, whereas differences between students accepted for degree and certificate courses were significant overall in the science subjects, there were no significant differences in the humanities and social science units.

Since there seems little reason to think that students who just pass, gaining two Es, differ appreciably from those who just fail - and may indeed, be inferior to students who gain, say, one B (4 points) and two failures by a narrow margin - perhaps some of these, too, could do well in degree courses if given the opportunity. Thus, despite the convenience to universities of selecting mainly on grade points, there seems to be considerable evidence favouring a more flexible policy. Certainly at the Associated College of Bradford University students (many of the mature) allowed to transfer from certificate courses to degree courses have proved a more than averagely successful group.

SUPPLEMENTARY TESTS AS PREDICTIVE MEASURES

In view of the rather poor predictive power of A-levels,
tests of intelligence and of aptitudes have been considered
as a possible addition.

Choppin and his associates outline results of an investigation into use of a Test of Academic Aptitude (TAA) as a
supplementary predictive measure for university applicants,
employing a similar structure to the American Scholastic
Aptitude Test (SAT); like SAT, it was designed to yield
two measures, namely verbal and mathematical aptitudes.
In the United States of America, the SAT has increased
multiple correlations of predictive measures with college
performance sometimes as high as 0.7.   In Britain, however, the similar TAA tests proved much less useful,
probably because students who sit for A-levels are already
highly selected, and those who apply to universities even
more so.   In the United States, there are no hurdles such
as the 11+ and O-levels, nor is there any screening in high
schools comparable with A-level examinations.

Thus, as we noted in Chapter 3, students reaching university or college in Britain almost all have the necessary
academic ability for degree courses.   As we have seen,
reasons for failure and withdrawal are more likely to relate
to personal problems or personality traits such as extroversion, neuroticism or psychotic tendencies or, alternatively, to dissatisfaction with courses.

An interesting finding in Australia (Pentony and Loftus,
1970), concerning use of intelligence tests in addition to
matriculatio results in selection for university, was that
mathematics entrants whose intelligence quotients were
higher relative to those of their peers than were their
mathematics leaving results tended to do poorly at university, whereas those who gained high mathematics matriculation scores and relatively lower intelligence quotients were
amongst the most successful students.   This confirms a
finding by A.W. Anderson (1960) that high scores in intelligence tests tended to be related with poor academic performance at Australian universities.

In Britain, Hudson (1964) reports similar findings: 24
per cent of future winners of open scholarships and exhibi-
tions fell within the bottom 30 per cent of his sample in IQ.
Future open scholars, he found, were distinguished not by
their test scores, but by their tendency to work hard, and
by the breadth of their interests outside the curriculum.

He cites illustrative examples of an outstanding young phys-
icist whose IQ was lower than some 80 per cent of his
class-mates and that of a brilliant young mathematician
whose IQ was just a little above average for his form.
Conceivably this may be because the intelligence test was a
verbal one. My own observation in a number of small
samples suggests that graduates in mathematics and physical sciences normally excel in Raven's Matrices Test, gaining between 60 and 65 of a possible 65 points, whereas
graduates in arts and social science perform less well in
this perceptual test of intelligence. Indeed, two arts
graduates from Oxford having first- or upper-second-class
degrees in English and philosophy obtained the quite
astonishingly poor scores of 28 and 33.

MEASURES OF PERSONALITY IN SELECTING STUDENTS?

During approximately the last ten years, attempts have been
made to add tests of personality to measures of attainment
and teachers' assessments, with a view to developing a
predictive measure based on all of these. Most of these
attempts have used either Eysenck's Personality Inventory
which gives measures of extroversion-introversion and of
stability-neuroticism, or Cattell's 16 Personality Factors
(16 PF) which provides sixteen interrelated measures of
personality characteristics; but the latter tests are brief
and have rather low reliability. Unfortunately, tests of
many personality variables prove unreliable in the sense
that there are marked variations in patterns of relationships
found in similar samples of individuals.

Nevertheless, as we noted in Chapter 3, there seems to
be substantial agreement that overall high neuroticism and
extroversion combine to inhibit academic achievement whilst
stability and introversion usually combine to promote success (Wankowski, 1973; Entwistle, 1972). However Warburton (1968) noted that the degree of introversion which
led to success differed with subject. In an extensive
study, so far unconfirmed, Entwistle et al. (1971) found
that neurotic introverts made good engineers, but stable
introverts did better in pure sciences. Neurotic introverts were also good at languages, but stable introverts
made better historians. Among social science students,
correlations between these personality dimensions and

attainment were near zero, confirming earlier findings.
Wankowski (1973) found the failure rate of stable introverts
in a physical science course was only 1 in 38 compared with
1 in 7 neurotic introverts (melancholics); but his sub-
samples were small.

Attempts to use personality variables in predicting success have also been made by Cattell and Butcher (1968).
A regression equation based on a measure of intelligence
together with Cattell's personality variables, resulted in a
high multiple correlation of 0.7, but as we have noted these
personality scales have poor reliability. The authors reported some relationship between attainment and measures
of conscientiousness, dominance, friendliness and depen-
dability.

A more relevant test may be the American Mehrabian
Need for Achievement Scale. Cohen, Reid and Boothroyd
(1973) who used this with British students in colleges of
education, found that the scale differentiated between students with high and low n'ach scores with respect to their
self-images, intellectual achievement, responsibility and
occupational aspirations. Conceivably, further experiment
with this scale, in combination with other measures, might
lead to improved predictions of student success. Nevertheless, as we have seen in Chapter 1, high need for
achievement may be satisfied in areas other than academic
ones. For this reason, attempts to devise tests of high
academic motivation have been made in the United States,
but Entwistle and Wilson (1977) report only moderately encouraging results.

OTHER VARIABLES AS PREDICTORS OF SUCCESS

Teachers who comment on lack of purpose in students may
be surprised that psychologists have rarely investigated
this dimension.

Two studies of students' goals have been made in Australia. Kearney (1969) found that students who had well-
defined, or fairly well-defined goals for the future did
about equally well in their courses, but those who could
not say what their goals were did significantly worse.
Pentony (1968), who studied a group of students in difficulties, noted a general lack of sense of purpose and direction; but all these students seemed to lack a happy relationship at home. Their energies he considered were ab-

sorbed in rebelling against dominating parents, struggling to free themselves from indulgent and possessive parents, or in withstanding homes which were places of discord and depression or which, whilst supplying meals and shelter, gave neither support nor sympathy.

In Britain, as we have noted in Chapter 5, Wankowski (1973) found, on comparing students who were very clearly and very poorly motivated concerning the future, that failure rate for the former was 1 in 41 whilst for the latter it rose to 1 in 6. Indeed amongst extremely poorly motivated male students, failure rate reached 1 in 2, and a similar rate of failure, i.e. 1 in 2, occurred amongst students of both sexes whose reasons for entering university were classed as indeterminate. A measure of motivation, comprising assessment of short- and long-term goals and reasons for entering university, correlated significantly with degree results, especially among commerce and social science male students and amongst stable and introverted female students.

It will be appreciated from the foregoing account of investigations that much remains to be explored and clarified before dependable predictive measures can be developed, if that ever proves possible. It is possible that a number of different measures may be needed for students entering different specialities.

Information about students which it might be useful to obtain when selecting entrants relates not only to academic performance but to 'need for achievement' in a general sense, their reasons for wishing to enter higher education, what they hope to do once qualified and, conceivably, some measure of extroversion and neuroticism. Levels of maturity, cognitive and learning styles, and orientations may be better explored after students are accepted. One aim of courses in higher education is to increase the level of students' maturity in thinking; whilst recognition of students' differences suggests options in courses and exercises rather than exclusion of certain kinds of applicant to any department, measures should be taken to ensure that extroverts who are accepted develop good study methods. In addition, students might be given more assistance in selecting a department congenial to their own aims and styles in learning.

Even a few tests may suffice to select well-motivated students, if these are well chosen and combined with skill in interviewing. Hudson (1968), for instance, used tests of 'divergent' thinking to identify students, lacking the usual

entry qualifications for university, who might do well in
degree courses. A majority of those who were allowed to
enter courses at Cambridge gained second-class degrees.
He has repeatedly made a plea for more flexibility in entry
qualifications into higher education since his study of creative workers and that of McClelland (1963) suggests that
some of them are likely to fail conventional measures of
attainment such as A-levels. They are also likely to withdraw from higher courses which allow little scope for ini-
tiative, invention or imagination or for the exercise of their
particular talents, whatever these may be. Thus, the response to their poor entry qualifications should not be to con-
sign them to a course of revision, but to provide revision
incidentally in a course of stimulating activities. One possibility is to set 'open-ended' experiments or projects in
science or engineering in which students are expected to
look up any knowledge they require.

Hudson's creative students who lacked A-levels may be
more mature versions of children in schools studied by
Wallach and Kogan (1965) who did relatively poorly in intelligence tests but excelled in tests of divergent thinking.
Unlike those who scored high on both measures, these children tended to be unpopular with both teachers and their
peers and to perform poorly in traditional schools; but they
blossomed in a stress-free, child-centred school environment, where they would choose some activities.

Other groups of school-leavers who may obtain qualifications which do not show their full promise include those who
have had their education disrupted by reorganization in
schools, or movement from school to school as a consequence of a parent's change of employment, those who
mature late, and, possibly, those having a bias to constructional, scientific and mathematical interests.

During the last fifteen or twenty years, until recently,
rapid turnover of teachers has resulted in some disruption
in teaching programmes, exposing pupils to a variety of
teaching methods and styles and the relatively poorer discipline which rapid changes sometimes entail. Reorganization in schools may also have taken its toll. It is, perhaps, not generally realized that many teachers enter new
experiments such as the introduction of comprehensive,
middle or upper schools without any special preparation by
way of courses or conferences; consequently, they will
probably have had no opportunity in advance to discuss the
aims of the new kind of school or to consider the different

attitudes towards, and expectations of, the different age or ability ranges in the school. Whatever their previous experience, whether in secondary, primary, grammar or modern schools, they are left to cope, possibly in some confusion and uncertainty unless there is enlightened direction from the head teacher who, equally, may have had no special preparation. Inevitably children's education suffers until the new system of schooling is established, especially if teachers feel so uncertain or confused that unnecessary mistakes are made. Local courses and conferences which follow, after a year or two, however well planned, are too late. Since at secondary school, in addition, there are serious shortages of well-qualified teachers in some subjects, notably English, mathematics and physics, it is more difficult than formerly to prepare pupils for success in examinations. If it is true that one-third of 'specialists' in mathematics, for instance, now have a qualification no higher than an O-level pass in the subject, it is, perhaps, astonishing how well the children do.

In primary schools, a further problem is that many teachers do not readily recognize the intellectual capacity in children whose talents show themselves in non-verbal ways Consequently, children whose interests are in construction, or scientific experiments and problems, and who make slow progress in reading and writing (perhaps because the topics offered do not appeal to them), may be judged stupid by teachers who do not have a good scientific or constructional background and so cannot offer stimulating work of this kind. Following a recent survey by HM inspectors of schools in 542 primary schools (DES, 1978), they report that the match with ability of work in science for the most able children of eleven years was satisfactory in less than a quarter of classes they observed, whilst art and craft and geography were at a suitable level for the most able in less than a third of classes. In contrast, the percentages for reading and mathematics were in the ranges 82-94 per cent and 75-84 per cent respectively. Where neglect of pupils' interests results in boredom or disruptive behaviour the result can be that their ability is underestimated so that they are consigned to lower streams; their potential may be unrecognized until too late for them to enter examination streams in secondary or upper school.

Similarly, late developers may be held back if at primary school slow progress and 'behaviour young for their age' give the impression of stupidity, whilst at secondary school

the burst of energy which follows with adolescence may
come too late for them to show their true potential in time
to enter examination streams at thirteen or fourteen.   The
comprehensive school system allows for this to some extent
since pupils may take O-levels in the sixth form, but it is
unlikely that they will achieve the two or three A-levels required for entry to universities and colleges.

Some pupils, especially boys, go to technical colleges
where they obtain ONC, HNC or HND qualifications which
enable them to proceed to university a year or so later than
their peers.   Those who join science and engineering
courses at the University of Bradford are usually found to
be highly motivated and to perform better than average.
Similarly, teachers who come to the university to take a
first degree as mature students prove highly motivated and
obtain good results in applied educational studies during
three years' part-time course.   Other mature students
qualify for advanced courses by obtaining Open University
degrees, sometimes quite late in life.

Thus, methods of increasing the numbers of motivated
students in universities and colleges depends on the flexibility of their teaching staff in accepting a proportion of
students having qualifications other than the usual two good
A-levels, in view of other evidence of motivation.   We have
already mentioned that Brown (1971) reported an experiment
in Ireland, where highly motivated intending teachers had
fewer failures than the better qualified students whose
courses they joined.

In the Associated Colleges of Bradford University in
1976 and 1977, all students entered the same Unit courses
in education initially, whether they were qualified only for
Certificate courses or had the necessary two A-levels to
enter degree courses.   There was considerable overlap in
performance between these groups.   Some of the best performances during the first and second years were by students who had passed only one A-level on entry, or in a
very few instances, none at all.   Mature students in particular often excelled.   Logic would suggest that all of
those who just qualified at the end of the second year should
have proceeded to the remaining two years of the honours
degree course if they wished to.   Caution prevailed, however, a considerably higher standard being required of
those who did not have the usual entrance qualifications.
Even this did not satisfy certain university teachers who
deemed this method of entry as necessarily implying a

'lowering of standards'. Of course, if poorly-qualified students entered some university courses it would be necessary to modify them during the first term or first year to enable these students to catch up, but there is no evidence that 'loss of standard', if any, applies to the abilities of the students, it applies rather to the level of their achievement at entry which may depend on teaching they received at school and, perhaps, late development. Indeed, where 'parallel' courses are run in some topics for well- and poorly-qualified students respectively during the first year, a considerable overlap in performance can be expected by the end of the year.

Two main conclusions follow. The first is that in attempting to find a greater number of students who are motivated to succeed it is reasonable to look at a rather wider population instead of depending exclusively on the administratively convenient requirement of two good A-levels. The second is that motivation of students in universities and colleges is largely a matter of suitability of courses to their varied needs, initial experiences which enable them to adjust to independence and study methods appropriate to higher education, to stimulating teaching and informative assessment of their performance.

In the first endeavour, both psychologists and teachers who are interested in such problems will continue to experiment in devising more informative methods of testing and interviewing applicants to select those who are motivated. In the second, motivation of students after they have been accepted depends mainly on the teachers. If students prove unmotivated, probably the first step is to find out more about their different needs, capabilities and interests; a second step might be to reconsider the course itself, especially the first term or first year, and to do so in discussion with students who as we have seen normally make perceptive and constructive comments; a third possibility is to reconsider teaching methods and the ways in which teachers interact with their students; whilst the fourth, and last, is to make sure that the methods of assessment both reinforce course aims and supply sufficient information to students to enable them to improve their performance. There is evidence to suggest that in these ways the motivation of many students can be increased.

References

ABERCROMBIE, M.L.J. (1970), 'Aims and techniques of group teaching' (3rd ed.) (Guildford, Society for Research into Higher Education).

ANDERSON, A.W. (1960), A note on high intelligence and low academic performance in the university, 'The Educand', 4 (1), 111-13.

BAGG, D.G. (1970), A-levels and university performance, 'Nature', 225 (21), March, 1105-8.

BARKE, R.J. (1969), Some preliminary data on the use of self evaluations and peer ratings in assigning university course grades, 'Journal of Educational Research', 62 (10), 444-8.

BEARD, R.M. (1969a), A conspectus of research and development in 'Assessment of undergraduate performance', report of a conference convened by the Committee of Vice-Chancellors and Principals and the Association of University Teachers, 27 March.

BEARD, R.M. (1969b), Methods of examining professional competence, 'Medical and Biological Illustrations', 19, (2), 127-8.

BEARD, R.M. (1976), 'Teaching and learning in higher education' (3rd ed.) (Harmondsworth, Penguin).

BEARD, R.M., LEVY, P.M. and MADDOX, H. (1964), Academic performance at university, 'Educational Review', 16 (3), 163-74.

BEARD, R.M. and POLE, K. (1971), Content and purpose of biochemistry examinations, 'British Journal of Medical Education', 5 (1), 13-21.

BEARD, R.M. and SENIOR, I. (1977), Initial experiences at university, 'Bulletin of Educational Research', 13 (1), Summer, 2-8.

BECKER, H.S., GEER, B. and HUGHES, E.C. (1968),
'Making the grade: the academic side of college life' (New
York, Wiley).
BLACK, P.J. (1968), University examinations, 'Physics
Education', 3 (2), 93-9.
BLACK, P.J., DYSON, N.A. and O'CONNOR, D.A. (1968),
Group Studies, 'Physics Education', 3 (6), 289-93.
BLIGH, D.A. (1971), 'What's the use of lectures?' (Har-
mondsworth, Penguin).
BLIGH, D.A. (1977), The Cynthia syndrome, 'Bulletin of
Educational Research', 13, 21-4.
BLIGH, D.A. et al. (1975), 'Teaching students' (Exeter
University Teaching Services).
BRISTOW, T. (1970), A reading seminar, 'The Library
College Journal' 3 (3), 13-22.
BRITISH MEDICAL STUDENTS' ASSOCIATION (1965),
'Report on medical education: suggestions for the future'
(British Medical Association).
BROCKBANK, J.P. (1968), Examining exams, 'The Times
Literary Supplement', no. 3465, 781-2.
BROCKBANK, J.P. (1969), New assessment techniques in
use - the arts, in 'Assessment of undergraduate perfor-
mance' (Universities Conference).
BROWN, G.A. (1971), The performance of non-graduate
student teachers in university courses, 'British Journal of
Educational Psychology', 41 (3), 314-16.
BRUNEL UNIVERSITY (1974), 'Industrial training for
degrees in technology' (Uxbridge, Brunel University).
BRUNER, J.S. (1966), 'Toward a theory of instruction'
(New York, Norton).
BURGESS, T. (1977), 'Education after school' (Harmonds-
worth, Penguin).
CATTELL, R.B. and BUTCHER, H.J. (1968), 'The predic-
tion of achievement and creativity' (New York, Bobbs-
Merrill).
CHOPPIN, B.H.L. and FARR (1972), 'After A-level? A
study of the transition from school to higher education'
(Slough, National Foundation for Educational Research).
CHOPPIN, B.H.L. et al. (1973), 'The prediction of aca-
demic success' (Slough, National Foundation for Educa-
tional Research).
CHOPPIN, B.H.L. and ORR, L. (1976), 'Aptitude testing
at 18+' (Slough, National Foundation for Educational Research).
CHRISTIE, T. and MILLS, J. (1973), 'The use of scholas-

tic aptitude test in university selection' (Department of Education, University of Manchester).

COHEN, L. (1972), Personality and changing problems among first year college of education students, 'Durham Research Review', 28, Spring, 617-22.

COHEN, L. and BATCOCK, A. (1969), Female university students and social influence, 'Educational Review', 21 (3), 234-41.

COHEN, L., REID, I. and BOOTHROYD, K. (1973), Validation of the Mehrabian Need for Achievement Scale with college of education students, 'British Journal of Educational Psychology', 43 (3), 269-73.

COHEN, L. and TOOMEY, D. (1973), Role orientations and sub-cultures among undergraduate students, 'Research in Education', 10 (1), 36-55.

COLLIER, K.G. (1969), Syndicate methods: further evidence and comment, 'Universities Quarterly', 23 (4), 431-6.

COOPER, B. and FOY, J.M. (1969), Students' study habits, attitudes and academic attainment, 'Universities Quarterly', 23 (2), 203-12.

COPE, R. (1971), 'An Investigation of Entrance Characteristics related to Types of College Dropouts' (Washington, DC, Office of Educational Reports).

CORNELIUS, M.L. (1972), The transition from school to university mathematics, 'Mathematical Gazette', October, 207-18.

COWAN, J. and MORTON, J. (1973), A structural game for undergraduates, 'Programmed learning and Educational Technology', 10 (4), 267-73.

COX, R. (1967), Examinations and higher education, 'Universities Quarterly', June, 21 (3), 292-340.

CRANDALL, V.J., PRESTON, A. and RABSON, A. (1960), Maternal reactions and the development of independence and achievement behaviour in young children, 'Child Development', 31, 243-51.

CROSSLEY, C.A. (1968), Tuition in the use of the library and of subject literature in the University of Bradford, 'Journal of Documentation', 24 (2), 91-7.

CROWN, S., LUCAS, C.T. and SUPRAMANIUM, S. (1973), The delineation and assessment of study difficulty in university students, 'British Journal of Psychiatry', 122 (4), 381-93.

CULLEN, J.B. (1973), Social identity and motivation, 'Psychological Reports', 33 (1), 338.

DAVIE, R.S. and RUSSELL, J.K. (1974), Attitudes and

abilities of cooperative students, 'Australian Journal of Education', 18 (2), 150–71.

DAVIE, R.S., DOYLE, K.J., RUSSELL, J.K. and STERN, W. (1975), 'Development of Cooperative Sandwich education', 4th report of the Commission on Advanced Education (Canberra, Australian Government Publishing Service).

DES (1978), 'Primary Education in England' (London, HMSO).

DOSKIN, V.A. and LAURENT'EVA, N.A. (1974), Rizm fiziologicheskikh funktsu: rezhim obucheniya (The rhythm of physiological functions and teaching arrangements), 'Vestnik vyssehisikoly', 5, 76–9.

ELTON, L.R.B. (1968), Success and failure in university physics courses, 'Physics Education', 3 (6), 323–9.

ENTWISTLE, N.J. (1972), Students and their academic performance in different types of institution, in Butcher, H.J. and Rudd, E. (eds), 'Contemporary problems in higher education' (Maidenhead, McGraw-Hill).

ENTWISTLE, N.J. and ENTWISTLE, D. (1970), The relationship between personality, study methods and academic performance, 'British Journal of Educational Psychology', 40 (2), 132–43.

ENTWISTLE, N.J., NISBET, J., ENTWISTLE, D. and COWELL, M.D. (1971), The academic performance of students, 'British Journal of Educational Psychology', 41 (3), 258–67.

ENTWISTLE, N.J. and BRENNAN, T. (1971), The academic performance of students II: types of successful students, 'British Journal of Educational Psychology', 41 (3), 268–76.

ENTWISTLE, N.J. and WILSON, J.D. (1977), 'Degrees of excellence: the academic achievement game' (London, Hodder & Stoughton).

EPSTEIN, H.J. (1970), 'A strategy for education' (Oxford University Press).

EPSTEIN, H.J. (1972), An experiment in education, 'Nature', Jan., 235 (5335), 203–5.

EVANS, L.R., INGERSOL, R.W. and SMITH, E.J. (1966), The reliability, validity and taxonomic structure of the oral examination, 'Journal of Medical Education', 41, 651–7.

EYSENCK, H.J. (1957), 'The dynamics of anxiety and hysteria' (Routledge & Kegan Paul).

EYSENCK, H.J. (1970), 'The structure of human personality' (Routledge & Kegan Paul).

FARRELL, M.J. and GILBERT, N. (1960), A type of bias in marking examination scripts, 'British Journal of Educational Psychology', 30 (1), 47-52.

FLOOD-PAGE, C. (1974), 'Student evaluation of teaching: the American experience' (Guildford, Society for Research into Higher Education).

GIBSON, J.N. (1970), The structure of intelligence, 'Bulletin of the British Psychological Society', 23 (81), 323-4.

GRUGEON, D. (ed.) (1973), 'Teaching by correspondence in the Open University' (Milton Keynes, Open University Press).

GUILFORD, J.P. (1956), The structure of intelligence, 'Psychological Bulletin', 53 (4), 267-94.

HALSTEAD, L.S. and GEERTSMA, R.H. (1973), The evaluation and selection of a medical school: a student perspective, 'British Journal of Medical Education', 7 (2), 94-9.

HELFER, R.E. and SLATER, C.H. (1971), Measuring the process of solving clinical diagnostic problems, 'British Journal of Medical Education', 5 (1), 48-52.

HENRY, J. (1977), The course tutor and project work, in 'Teaching at a distance', No. 9 (Milton Keynes, Open University Press).

HIMMELWEIT, H.T. (1963), Student selection: Implications derived from two student selection enquiries, in Halmos, K.P. (ed.), 'Sociological studies in British university education' (University of Keele).

HIRST, K. and BIGGS, N. (1969), Undergraduate projects in mathematics, 'Educational Studies in Mathematics', 1 (3), 252-61.

HOLLOWAY, P.J. (1966), The effect of lecture time on learning, 'British Journal of Educational Psychology', 31, (3), 255-8.

HORNSBY-SMITH, M.P. (1973), Styles of teaching and their influence upon the interests of students in science, 'Durham Research Review', 7 (31), 807-15.

HOWELL, S.H. (1971), A study of educational and personality factors of students (Department of Mathematical Statistics, University of Birmingham, unpublished MSc dissertation).

HOUSTON, J.G. and PILLINER, A.E. (1974), The effect of verbal teaching style on the attainment of educational objectives in physics, 'British Journal of Educational Psychology', 44 (2), 163-73.

HUDSON, L. (1964), Future open scholars, 'Nature', 202 (4934), 834.

HUDSON, L. (1966), 'Contrary imaginations' (London, Methuen).

HUDSON, L. (1968), 'Frames of mind' (London, Methuen).

HUDSON, L. (1970, ed.), The ecology of human intelligence, ch. 17, 'Academic prediction' (Harmondsworth, Penguin).

JEPSON, J. (1969), Some methods of teaching practical biochemistry, in Wills, E.D. (ed.), 'Practical biochemistry in the medical course' (report of the Federal European Biochemical Society Summer School, April 1968).

JEVONS, F.R. (1970), Liberal studies in science – a successful experiment, 'Education in Chemistry', 7 (3), 88–9.

KANDEL, I. (1936), Examinations and their substitutes in the United States, in Carnegie Foundation for the Advancement of Teaching, 'Bulletin 28' (New York, Carnegie Foundation).

KATZ, F.M. and KATZ, C.N. (1967), Occupational aspirations of university students, 'Australian Journal of Higher Education', 3 (1), 8–19.

KATZ, F.M. and KATZ, C.N. (1968), Students' definition of the objectives of a university education, 'Australian Journal of Higher Education', 3 (2), 111–18.

KEARNEY, J.E. (1969), Success factors in tertiary education, 'Australian Journal of Higher Education', 3 (3), 231–7.

KELLER, F.S. (1968), Good-bye teacher ..., 'Journal of Applied Behaviour Analysis', 1 (1), 78–89.

KENDALL, M.N. (1964), Those who failed. 1: The further education of former students, 'Universities Quarterly', 18 (4), 398–406.

KENDALL, M.N. (1973), Report on a survey of students prematurely terminating their university courses in 1968–9 and 1969–70 (London, Research Unit for Student Problems, unpublished).

KENNEL, J.H., TEMPIO, C.R. and WILE, M.Z. (1973), Self evaluation by first year medical students in a chemical programme, 'British Journal of Medical Education', 7 (4), 230–8.

KENNET, K.F. and CROPLEY, A.J. (1975), Uric acid and divergent thinking: a possible relationship, 'British Journal of Psychology', 66 (2), 175–80.

KING, W.H. (1973), A prediction from A–level performance of university degree performance, 'Physics Education', 8 (2), 106–7.

KOGUT, M. (1975), Survey of biochemical topics used by clinicians in teaching and practice, 'British Journal of Medical Education', 9 (3), 188–94.

LA NAUZE, J.A. (1940), 'Some aspects of educational opportunity in S. Australia' (Melbourne, Australian Educational Studies).

LAVACH, J.F. (1973), The effect of arousal on short- and long-term memory, 'Journal of Educational Research', 67 (3), 131-3.

LEWIN, K. (ed.) (1952),'Field theory in social science: selected theoretical papers' (Tavistock).

LINN, B.S., AROSTEGUI, M. and ZEPPA, R. (1975), Performance rating scale for peer and self assessments, 'British Journal of Medical Education', 9 (2), 98-102.

LOEWENTHAL, K. and KOSTREVSKI, B. (1973), The effects of training in written communication of verbal skills, 'British Journal of Educational Psychology', 43 (1), 82-6.

MCCLELLAND, D.C. (1958), The importance of early learning in the formation of motives, in Atkinson, J.W. (ed.), 'Motives in fantasy, action and society' (Princeton, Van Nostrand).

MCCLELLAND, D.C. (1963), The calculated risk: an aspect of scientific performance, in Gruber, H.E. (ed.), 'Scientific Creativity: its recognition and development' (New York, Atherton).

MCCLELLAND (1961-70), 'The achieving society' (New York, Free Press; London, Macmillan).

MACKINNON, D.W. (1962), The nature and nurture of creative talent, 'American Psychologist', 17, 484.

MCKEVITT, O. (1969), Orientations and behaviour patterns of university student sub-cultures, 'Australian Journal of Higher Education', 3 (3), 210-17.

MCVEY, P.J. (1975), The errors in marking examination scripts in electrical engineering, 'International Journal of Electrical Engineering Education', 12 (3), 203-16.

MALLESON, N. (1976), Students leaving mechanical engineering courses, 'Universities Quarterly', 22 (1), 74-88.

MARRIS, P. (1964), 'The experience of higher education', (Routledge & Kegan Paul).

MILLER, C.M.L. (1976), Intellectual development, confidence and assessment, in Klug, E. (ed.), 'A Question of Degree' (Slough, NFER).

MILLER, C.M.L. and PARLETT, M. (1974), 'Up to the mark: a study of the examination game' (Guildford, Society for Research into Higher Education).

MORTON, J.B. and MACBETH, W.A.A.G. (1977), Correlations between staff, peer and self assessments of fourth-year students of surgery, 'Medical Education', 11 (3), 171-4.

MOSS, H.A. and KAGAN, J. (1961), Stability of achievement and recognition seeking behaviours from early childhood through adulthood, 'Journal of Abnormal and Social Psychology', 62 (3), 504–13.

MUSGROVE, F. (1969), What worries students, 'Educational Research', November, 12 (1), 56–9.

NATKIN, E. and GOULD, R.E. (1967), Evaluation of preclinical laboratory performance, 'Journal of Dental Education', 31 (2), 152–61.

NUFFIELD FOUNDATION (1974), 'Newsletter', no. 5 (London, Nuffield Lodge, Regents Park).

NUFFIELD FOUNDATION (1976), 'Newsletter', no. 7 (London, Nuffield Lodge, Regents Park).

O'CONNELL, S. (1970), From school to university, 'Universities Quarterly', 24 (2), 177–88.

O'CONNELL, S., WILSON, A.W. and ELTON, L.R.B. (1969), A pre-knowledge survey for university science students, 'Nature', 222 (5193), 526.

PARLETT, M.R. (1970), The syllabus–bound student, in Hudson, L., 'The ecology of human intelligence' (Harmondsworth, Penguin).

PARLETT, M.R. and KING, J.G. (1971), 'Concentrated study: a pedagogic innovation observed ' (Guildford, Society for Research into Higher Education).

PARKE, R.D. (ed.) (1969), 'Readings in social development' (New York, Holt, Rinehart & Winston).

PENTONY, P. (1968), A study of students in academic difficulties, 'Australian Journal of Higher Education', 3 (2), 179–85.

PENTONY, P. and LOFTUS, A.R.T. (1970), On prediction of the first year performance of science students from I.Q. and performance in matriculation examination, 'Australian Journal of Higher Education', 4 (1), 57–64.

PERRY, W.G. (1968), 'Forms of intellectual and ethical development in the college years: a scheme' (New York, Holt, Rinehart & Winston).

PETCH, J.A. (1961), 'G.C.E. and Degree I' (Manchester, Northern Universities Joint Matriculation Board).

PETCH, J.A. (1963), 'G.C.E. and Degree II' (Manchester, Northern Universities Joint Matriculation Board).

PETERS, R. (1958), 'The Concept of Motivation' (London, Routledge & Kegan Paul).

POSTLETHWAIT, S.N., NOVAK, J. and MURRAY, H.T. (1964), 'An integrated experience approach to learning' (Minneapolis, Burgess Publishing Co.).

POWELL, J.L. (1973), 'Selection for University in Scotland' (Edinburgh, Scottish Council for Research in Education).

PROSSER, A.P. (1967), Oral reports on laboratory work, in 'Teaching for efficient learning', report of a conference held at the University of London Institute of Education, January (University Teaching Methods Unit).

ROE, A. (1953), A psychological study of eminent psychologists and anthropologists, and a comparison with biological and physical scientists, 'Psychological Monographs', 67, no. 352.

ROGERS, J. (1977), 'Adult Learning' (2nd ed.) (Harmondsworth, Penguin).

ROSEN, B.C. and D'ANDRADE, R. (1959), The psychological origins of achievement motivation, 'Sociometry', 22, 185-218.

ROSENSHINE, B. (1971), 'Teaching behaviours and student achievement', IEA Studies no. 6 (Slough, National Foundation for Educational Research).

ROSS, D. (1972-7), 'Courses in legal practice' (Melbourne, Leo Cussen Institute for Continuing Legal Education).

ROWNTREE, D. (1976), 'Learn how to study' (2nd ed.) (London, Macdonald & Jane's).

RUDDOCK, J. (1978), 'Learning through group discussion: a study of seminar work in higher education' (Guildford, Society for Research intoHigher Education).

SAUNDERS, M. et al. (1969), 'Report of the Commission on Teaching in Higher Education' (London, National Union of Students).

SAVAGE, R.D. (1972), An exploratory study of individual characteristics associated with attainment in medical school, 'British Journal of Medical Education', 6 (1), 68-77.

SILCOCK, A. (1965), An investigation into possible relationships between reading ability scores and university first year examination results, 'Australian Journal of Higher Education', 2 (2), 113-18.

SMALL, J.J. (1966), 'Achievement and adjustment in the first year at university' (Wellington, New Zealand, Council for Educational Research).

SMITH, A.D. and JEPSON, J.B. (1972), Variation of the information game for use in a preclinical biochemistry course, 'The Lancet', 2, September 16, 585-6.

SMITHERS, A.G. (1976), 'The Sandwich course: an integrated experience?' (Slough, National Foundation for Educational Research).

SNOW, C.P. (1959), 'The two cultures and the scientific revolution' (Cambridge University Press).

SNYDER, B.R. (1973), 'The hidden curriculum' (Boston, MIT Press).

SPENCE, K.W. (1959), The relation of learning theory to the technique of education, 'Harvard Educational Review', 29, 84-95.

STEADMAN, S.D. (1973), Immaturity: The common trait of early leavers, 'Times Higher Education Supplement', 75, (23 March), 13.

STEEDMAN, W. (1974), The chemical literature: an undergraduate course, 'Education in Chemistry', 11 (3) 93.

STEUBNER, E.A. and JOHNSON, R.P. (1969), A hospital clerkship programme for dental students: an exploratory study, 'Journal of Dental Education', 33 (2), 224-9.

STEWART, D. (ed.) (1977), 'Teaching for the Open University' (Milton Keynes, Open University Press).

STUDENTS' SOCIETY COMMITTEE OF ROYAL DENTAL HOSPITAL SCHOOL OF DENTAL SURGERY (1966), Report on opinion poll on the lecture courses, supplement to 'Extract', 33.

TAYLOR, J.L. (1971), 'Instructional planning systems: a gaming simulation approach to urban problems' (Cambridge University Press).

TAYLOR, J.L. and WALFORD, R. (1978), 'Learning and the simulation game' (Milton Keynes, Open University Press).

TAYLOR, R.G. and HANSON, G.R. (1969), Pre-college mathematics workshop and freshmen achievement, 'Journal of Educational Research', 64 (3), 157-60.

TINTO, V. (1975), Dropout from higher education: a theoretical synthesis of recent research, 'Review of Educational Research', 45 (1), 89-135.

UNIVERSITY GRANTS COMMITTEE (1968), 'An Enquiry into student progress' (London, HMSO).

UNIVERSITY OF LONDON, UNIVERSITY TEACHING METHODS UNIT (1976), 'Improving teaching in higher education' (UTMU).

VENESS, T. (1968), Developments in social psychology, 'Penguin Social Science Survey' (Harmondsworth, Penguin).

WALFORD, R. (1972), in 'Games and Simulations' (London, BBC Publications).

WALLACH, M. and KOGAN, N. (1965), A new look at the creativity-intelligence distinction, in Vernon, P.E. (ed.), 'Creativity' (Harmondsworth, Penguin).

WANKOWSKI, J.A. (1972), Student wastage: the Birmingham experience, in Butcher, H.J. and Rudd, E. (eds), 'Contemporary problems in higher education' (McGraw-Hill).

WANKOWSKI, J.A. (1973), 'Temperament, motivation and academic achievement' (2 vols) (University of Birmingham Educational Survey).

WARBURTON, F. (1968), Personality factors and academic success (University of Manchester, unpublished manuscript).

WASON, P.C. (1970), On writing scientific papers, 'Physics Bulletin', 21 (9), 407-8.

WHITELAND, J.W.R. (1966), The selection of research students, 'Universities Quarterly', 21 (1), 44-7.

WILLIS, F., DOBLE, G., SANKARAYYA, U. and SMITHERS, A. (1977), 'Residence abroad and the student of modern languages' (University of Bradford Modern Languages Centre).

WILSON, J.D. (1971), Predicting levels of first year university performance, 'British Journal of Educational Psychology', 41 (2), 167-70.

WOODFORD, F.D. (1972), Experiences in teaching scientific writing in the U.S.A., 'Journal of Biological Education', 6 (1), 9-12.

WRIGHT, E. (1968), A research project for clinical medical students, in 'Innovations and experiments in university teaching methods', pp. 70-3 (University of London Institute of Education, University Teaching Methods Unit, January).

YOUNG, S. and GILLESPIE, G. (1972), Experience with the multiple-choice paper in the primary fellowship examination in Glasgow, 'British Journal of Medical Education', 6 (1), 44-52.

Index